# Complete English for Cambridge Secondary 1

Series editor: Dean Roberts
Annabel Charles
Alan Jenkins
Tony Parkinson

Oxford excellence for Cambridge Secondary 1

OXFORD

OXFORD
UNIVERSITY PRESS

Great Clarendon Street, Oxford, OX2 6DP, United Kingdom

Oxford University Press is a department of the University of Oxford. It furthers the University's objective of excellence in research, scholarship, and education by publishing worldwide. Oxford is a registered trade mark of Oxford University Press in the UK and in certain other countries



First published in 2016



British Library Cataloguing in Publication Data
Data available

978-0-19-836466-5

11

Paper used in the production of this book is a natural, recyclable product made from wood grown in sustainable forests.
The manufacturing process conforms to the environmental regulations of the country of origin.

Printed in Great Britain by Bell and Bain Ltd, Glasgow

**Acknowledgements**
The publishers would like to thank the following for permissions to use their photographs:

Cover image: David Newton/Bridgeman Art; p2l: © RubberBall/Alamy Stock Photo; p2r: Anna Hoychuk/Shutterstock; p3: Bildagentur Zoonar GmbH/Shutterstock; p4: Volodymyr Herasymchuk/Shutterstock; p8: Oleksiy Mark/Shutterstock; p15: Photographee.eu/Shutterstock; p2: Radu Bercan/Shutterstock; p16: v.schlichting/Shutterstcok; p18: Cuson/Shutterstock; p18l: © theatrepix/Alamy Stock Photo; p22: © Lynn Goldsmith/AS400 DB/Corbis/Image Library; p27: © Nature Photographers Ltd/Alamy Stock Photo; p29: © Adam Woolfitt/Corbis/Image Library; p32: Cuson/Shutterstock; p34: Christian Lagerek/Shutterstock; p34l: © VIEW press/Demotix/Corbis/Image Library; p34r: Nardus Engelbrecht/Gallo Images/Getty Images; p36: catwalker/Shutterstock; p37: totallyPic.com/Shutterstock; p41: Horst Lieber/Shutterstock; p42: stocksolutions/Shutterstock; p43: ducu59us/Shutterstock; p44: michaeljung/Shutterstock; p48: enterphoto/Shutterstock; p50: Anan Kaewkhammul/Shutterstock; p50l: Marcel Jancovic/Shutterstock; p50r: © All Canada Photos/Alamy Stock Photo; p51: Claudio Bertoloni/Shutterstock; p52: Guenter Guni/iStock; p53: © Chris Fredriksson/Alamy Stock Photo; p56: PatrickPoendl/iStock; p57: The Visual Explorer/Shutterstock; p59: Weerawit Thitiworasith/Shutterstock; p60bl: © Nature Picture Library/Alamy Stock Photo; p60t: © Kip Evans/Alamy Stock Photo; p60br: © Martin Harvey/Alamy Stock Photo; p64: Anan Kaewkhammul/Shutterstock; p66: Sebastian Duda/Shutterstock; p66l: Hero Images/Getty Images; p66r: S.Pytel/Shutterstock; p71: Shutterstock; p72: Jack.Q/Shutterstock; p74: STAFF/AFP/Getty Images; p75: © Omar Martinez/Fotoarena/Corbis/Image Library; p76: © Henry Westheim Photography/Alamy Stock Photo; p80: Sebastian Duda/Shutterstock; p82: Daniel Prudek/Shutterstock; p82l: © Stefano Cavoretto/Alamy Stock Photo; p82r: lculig/Shutterstock; p84: Daniel Prudek/Shutterstock; p87: s5iztok/iStock; p88: mady70/Shutterstock; p91: wacomka/Shutterstock; p92: Andrej Glucks/Shutterstock; p93: SasinT/Shutterstock; p96: Stokkete/Shutterstock; p98: George Clerk/iStock; p98l: saiko3p/Shutterstock; p98r: Beowulf fights with the dragon, illustration from 'Stories of Legendary Heroes' (colour litho), Brock, Henry Matthew (1875-1960) / Private Collection / Bridgeman Images; p99: Catherine Lane/iStock; p102: Vasily Gureev/Shutterstock; p103: Matyas Rehak/Shutterstock; p105: Rich Carey/Shutterstock; p109: alexkatkov/Shutterstock; p110: © AF archive/Alamy Stock Photo; p110bl: Lana Stem/Shutterstock; p111: Artisticco/Shutterstock; p112: George Clerk/iStock; p114: slhy/Shutterstock; p114l: © Corbis/Image Library; p114r: © DOD Photo/Alamy Stock Photo; p120: Christophe Cerisier/E+/Getty Images; p121: Laurin Rinder/Shutterstock; p125: © National Geographic Creative/Alamy Stock Photo; p128: Annette Shaff/Shutterstock; p130: De-V/Shutterstock; p130l: © ImagesBazaar/Alamy Stock Photo; p130r: Rob Lewine/Getty Images; p131: Steve Debenport/iStock; p132: Hurst Photo/Shutterstock; p134: Randrei/Shutterstock; p135l: Maria Skaldina/Shutterstock; p135r: Richard Whitcombe/Shutterstock; p136: Joana Lopes/Shutterstock; p140: Mzansi Youth Choir; p144: Fiona Ayerst/Shutterstock; End matter: David Wyatt.

Artwork by Six Red Marbles and OUP.

The author and publisher are grateful for permission to reprint extracts from the following copyright material:

**Isaac Asimov**: *The Robots of Dawn* (Doubleday, 1983), copyright © 1983 by Nightfall, Inc, reproduced by permission of the publishers, HarperCollins Publishers Ltd and Doubleday, an imprint of the Knopf Doubleday Publishing Group, a division of Penguin Random House LLC. All rights reserved.

**Khaled Hosseini**: *And the Mountains Echoed* (Bloomsbury, 2013), copyright © Khaled Hosseini 2013, reproduced by permission of Bloomsbury Publishing Plc.

**Timo Kaphengst** and **Lucy Smith**: 'The Impact of Biotechnology on Developing Countries', Briefing, edited by the European Parliament, February 2013, http://www.europarl.europa.eu/RegData/etudes/note/join/2013/433806/EXPO-DEVE_NT(2013)433806_EN.pdf, copyright © European Union 2013,reproduced by permission of the authors and of the European Parliament.

**Bobbi Katz**: 'Drifting' from *Trailblazers: Poems of Exploration* by Bobbi Katz (Greenwillow Books, 2007), copyright © Bobbi Katz 1997, 2001, 2007, reproduced by permission of the author.

**Gill Lewis**: *Sky Hawk* (OUP, 2011), text copyright © Gill Lewis 2011, with illustrations by Mark Owen, reproduced by permission of Oxford University Press.

**Patrick Ness**: opening of *A Monster Calls* (Walker, 2011), copyright © Patrick Ness 2011, reproduced by permission of Walker Books Ltd, London SE11 5HJ, www.walker.co.uk.

**Wilfred Noyce**: 'Breathless' from *South Col: One man's adventure on the ascent of Everest* (Heinemann, 1954), copyright © The Estate of Wilfred Noyce 1954, reproduced by permission of Johnson & Alcock Ltd.

**R J Palacio**: opening of *Wonder* (Bodley Head, 2013), reproduced by permission of The Random House Group Ltd.

**Slamovir Rawicz**: *The Long Walk: the true story of a trek to freedom* (Robinson, 2007), reproduced by permission of the publishers, Little, Brown Book Group Ltd.

**Meg Rosoff**: *How I Live Now* (Penguin, 2004), copyright © Meg Rosoff 2004, reproduced by permission of the publishers, Penguin Books Ltd and Penguin Random House LLC.

# Contents

# Introduction to Student Book 8

Welcome to Oxford's **Complete English for Cambridge Secondary 1 Student Book**. This book and the student workbook will support you and your teacher as you engage with Stage 8 of the Cambridge curriculum framework.

It aims to encourage you in becoming:

- **Confident** in your English skills and your ability to express yourself
- **Responsible** for your own learning and responsive to and respectful of others
- **Reflective** as a learner so that you can be a life-long learner – not just in school now
- **Innovative** and ready for new challenges as global citizen
- **Engaged** in both academic and social situations.

## Student book and Workbook

There are some great features in your book. Here's an explanation of how they work.

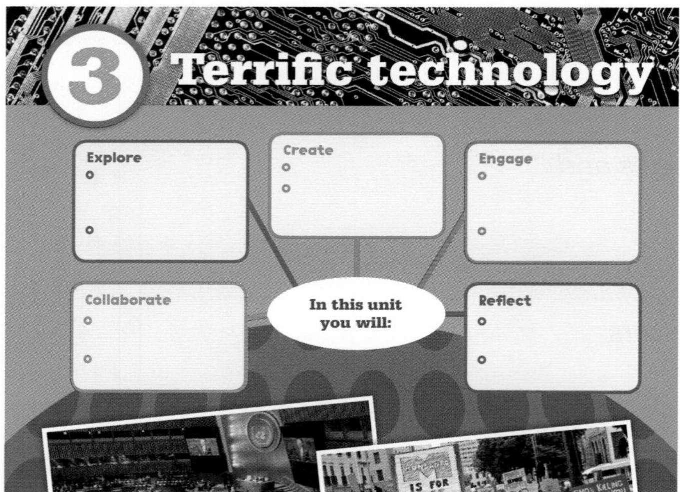


At the start of every unit, you'll see this diagram above. It gives you a quick summary of what the unit will be about and what kind of activities you'll engage with.

Each unit has a global theme. You'll explore science, technology and the impact of biotechnology in Unit 3, *Terrific technology*. Visit jungles, deserts and other hostile environments in *Unnatural nature* and find out about world myths and legends in *Heroic history*.

Through the Thinking time and Speaking and listening features you get the chance to express what you already know about a topic, think critically and find out more from your classmates whilst exploring new ideas.

This leads on to readings from modern and pre-twentieth century non-fiction, media texts, news articles and genre fiction. Comprehension tasks help you demonstrate your understanding of explicit and implicit meaning and lead from information retrieval to generating new ideas and material. Texts are accompanied by language acquisition and consolidation activities, spelling and grammar activities.

**Glossary**

Use the Word clouds to learn new vocabulary, exploring meanings and usage in context. The Glossary will help you with words or phrases that you may not find in a dictionary because they are uncommon, colloquial or technical phrases.

## Vocabulary

Learning new words and perhaps more importantly, learning exactly how they should be used is a key element of this series of books. There are lots of *word building* exercises for you to extend and enhance your vocabulary. Some new words you will meet in Stage 8 are: carbohydrate, nutritious, multifarious, unprecedented, iconic, sustainability, debacle, elliptical, malevolent, independent, scant, tradition, ancient, primitive, fantasy, ecology, infinitesimal, gawking, and intonation. Well done if you already know some of these. Don't worry if you don't - it's our aim to help you build up your vocabulary.

## Listening

You will listen to a radio discussion about healthy eating, an interview with an artistic director discussing the world tour of a stage play, a talk by a wildlife photographer, and a lively discussion about books and what makes a good story. When you listen to all of these people, and more, you will be practising your skills of listening to locate details, listening to understand the gist of what is being said, and listening to make inferences… trying to work out what people really mean!

### Language development

When the opportunities arise, we have incorporated language learning activities for you. We hope that these language awareness and language development activities will help improve your grammar, spelling and punctuation. In this Stage 8 book there is a focus on stylistic techniques, sentence structure and paragraphs, verbs and verb tenses, using images, similes, and metaphors to good effect, describing locations and creating atmosphere through setting, developing techniques for creating character, creating positive and negative bias in your writing, using a wide range of technical and specialist language, exploring prefixes.

## Writing

Every unit has a writer's workshop where you will learn skills of writing for different purposes linked to some of the texts you have read in the unit. Stage 8 includes; creating an information leaflet on eating healthily and designing a healthy drink or snack, writing a speech on artificial intelligence, writing a report for a school magazine and an article for a newspaper, writing a story about a superhero. With step by step guidance, you will develop the structure and organize your ideas using a range of sentences and presentations for particular effects.

### Reflecting and checking progress

**Progress check** 

## Reflecting on your learning

Being a responsible learner means discovering your progress and planning what you need to do to improve and move forward. Workbook 8 enables you to practise and expand on what you've been doing in lessons independently or for homework.

Each unit ends with a quick, fun quiz as a 'progress check' and a personal reflection so that you can understand your own personal development in English.

# 1 Foodies' delight

**In this unit you will:**

**Explore**
- how to encourage young people to eat healthily
- the use of paragraphs in structuring ideas

**Create**
- an information sheet about healthy eating
- a letter promoting a healthy drink or snack

**Engage**
- with whether a wide choice of foods is healthy or unhealthy
- with how to improve your spelling

**Collaborate**
- to devise a healthy drink or snack
- to produce a television advertisement

**Reflect**
- on your favourite food
- how to use a range of sentences

I choose some foods because I like the pictures or words on the packet.

I choose food that I enjoy and food that is good for me.

I like all foods, as long as they contain chocolate.

## Thinking time

Some people say there is too much choice these days.

1. Do you have a wide variety of food to choose from? Would you like more or less choice, and why?
2. What is your favourite food? What do you like about it?
3. What is the food you like least, and why?
4. We are often told what we should and should not eat for our health. Do you think it is up to each person to decide, or should people be given advice on what to eat?

## Speaking and listening – a matter of choice

Discuss the quotations on page 2. Do you make similar food choices? Share experiences of when you had a choice of food. Take it in turns to answer these questions:

- What foods could you choose from?
- Where were you?
- Who cooked or prepared the foods?
- What did you choose?
- Why did you choose those foods?
- Do you think you make the right food choices? Why?

Discuss your choices and reasons.

Strawberry
400 ml
Two+one
Up to 5 flavors
Up to 5 flavors
Buy 2 Get 1
FREE
Fruit-nut
Choco-nut
CHOOSE FROM 41 FLAVOURS!

# A blog about food choices

http://foodiesdelight.wordpress.com

## Spoilt for choice

Do you know how many kinds of breakfast **cereal** there are in my local supermarket? 165 kinds. Yes, 165! – and that's just one product. Think about all the **varieties** of biscuits, yoghourt, chocolate bars, soup. We have so much choice these days, it's incredible!

So all this choice must be a good thing, right? It makes us happier, right? Well, **not necessarily**. People like the idea of having a choice, and many people think more choice must be a good thing. But, in fact, too much choice can cause us problems.

If there are too many different things to choose from, we can become **paralysed** with **indecision** and not know what to choose. If you offer me a choice of three cookies, I can decide fairly quickly which one I want. But if you offer me a choice of 33 cookies, my brain can't cope. It feels like a computer given too much data to process and it crashes!

Another problem with too much choice is we think that somewhere there must be the *perfect* cookie. The fact is, there isn't – so when we have spent half an hour deciding which cookie we want, we feel disappointed, because it's not as good as we expected it to be. It's not cookie **perfection**. And then we begin to regret all the other cookies we didn't choose, thinking one of them might have been better.

So there *can* be such a thing as *too* much choice. According to Barry Schwartz, who has written a book about choice, we need to recognise that while some choice is good, too much can make us confused and **discontented**. He argues we should focus on being pleased with what we choose. I am going to remember this next time I'm offered a cookie – choose one and enjoy it!

## Understanding

1. How many different types of breakfast cereal are there in the writer's local supermarket?
2. Why do many people think the more choice the better?
3. Explain in your own words why having too many choices can be problematic.
4. How do you know the blog writer is an expert on the subject?
5. What is his solution to the problem?

| | |
|---|---|
| cereal | paralysed |
| discontented | perfection |
| indecision | varieties |
| not necessarily | |

Key concept

### Word families

All words belong to families. There are different types of word families.

One type of word family involves words that come from the same root word. For example, the word 'discontented' comes from the root word 'content'.

content
contented
contentedly
contentment
contentedness
discontent
discontented
discontentedly
discontentment
discontentedness

## Word builder

**Create a word family for two more of the words from the Word cloud.** Share your ideas with others in your class.

## Developing your language – stylistic techniques

In this blog, the writer uses a number of techniques to keep the reader interested.

**Answer the following questions.**

1. Match each technique to a quotation from the blog.

| Technique the writer uses |
|---|
| **a.** Question to engage the reader's interest |
| **b.** Use of facts and figures |
| **c.** Use of simile |
| **d.** Use of opinion |
| **e.** Use of first person plural |
| **f.** An exclamation |

| Example from the blog |
|---|
| 'it's incredible!' |
| 'we think that somewhere there must be the *perfect* cookie' |
| 'It makes us happier, right?' |
| '165 kinds' |
| 'all this choice must be a good thing' |
| 'like a computer given too much data to process' |

2. Write the opening of your own blog about a topic you feel strongly about.

   Aim to write at least five sentences. Try to include at least three of the techniques you looked at above.

**Remember**

Similes compare a person or a thing to something else, using words such as *like* and *as*.

## Sentences and sentence punctuation

**Answer the following questions.**

1. Which of the following are complete sentences?
   - **a** Where the cook is now.
   - **b** Sit down at the end of the dining room.
   - **c** Running into the kitchen, screaming.
   - **d** Although it was incredibly wet and rainy on the day of the cookery competition.
2. Now turn the 'sentences' which are incomplete into complete sentences. You will need to add words.
3. Which type of sentence is each of the following?
   - **a** Fish is a good source of protein.
   - **b** If you learn to cook, you can make dinner for the family.
   - **c** My favourite food is a banana split, with chocolate and salted caramel ice cream, strawberries, and whipped cream.
   - **d** After you have chosen your dessert, try not to regret your choice.
   - **e** Would you like to eat dinner or see round the city first?
4. Use the phrases, clauses, and conjunctions below to write:
   - **a** two simple sentences
   - **b** two compound sentences
   - **c** two complex sentences.
5. Construct a grammatically accurate sentence using as many of the phrases and clauses below as you can.

**Remember**

Simple sentences have one clause. Compound and complex sentences have two or more clauses. Clauses are joined by a coordinating conjunction (e.g. *and*) or subordinating conjunction (e.g. *although*).

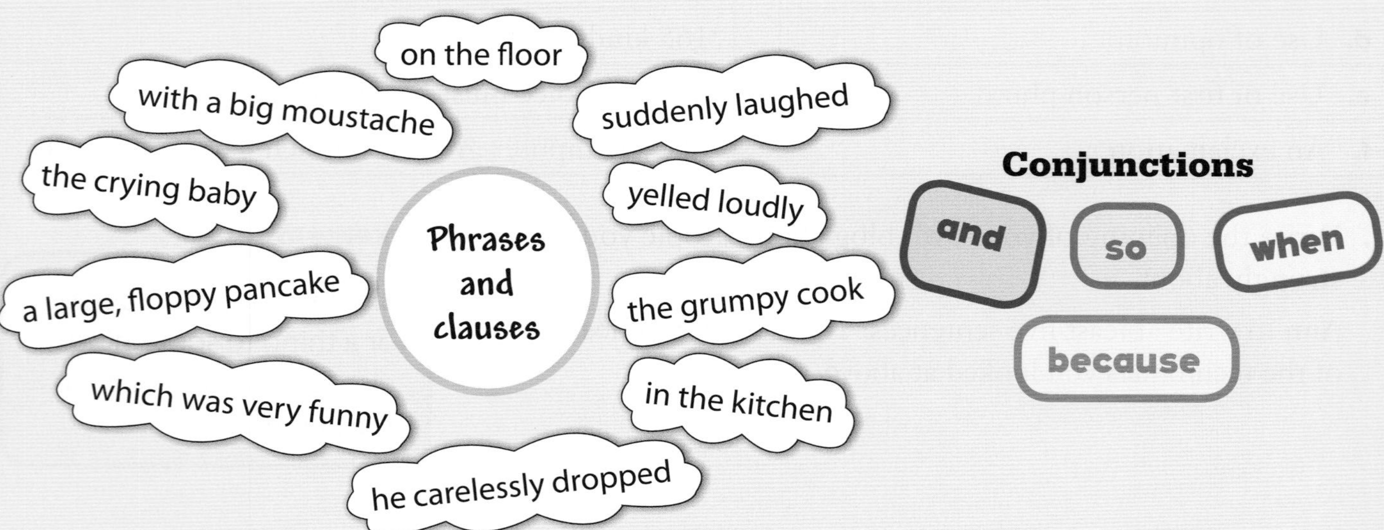


**Conjunctions**

and | so | when | because

Key concept

**Parenthetical phrases**

A parenthetical phrase is a phrase that has been added into a sentence which is already complete, to provide additional information. It is usually separated from other clauses using a pair of commas or a pair of brackets (parentheses). Example:

The goods train*, already late by five minutes,* was carrying milk.

## Punctuation – commas for parenthesis

**Answer the following questions.**

1. Find the parenthetical phrase in the sentences below.
   - **a** Shanghai, famous for its steamed crab, is one of the largest cities in China.
   - **b** In 2013, the Red Café, based at Manchester United football ground, won tourist attraction of the year.
   - **c** Elephants, highly intelligent animals with a remarkable memory, eat 300 kilograms of vegetation a day.
   - **d** In 2012, chefs in Rome baked, using 4,000 kilograms of mozzarella cheese, the world's largest pizza, according to the World Record Academy.
2. Add parenthetical phrases to the sentences below.
   - **a** It is important to eat at least five portions of fruit and vegetables every day.
   - **b** Shopping is my favourite pastime.
   - **c** Penang is in Malaysia.
   - **d** Come to Crest Café for an amazing meal!

**Read the following article about the quantity of sugar in fizzy drinks.**

# Are children consuming too much sugar?

Children are consuming **staggering** amounts of sugar every time they have a soft drink, health experts warn.

Everyday favourites contain the same amount of sugar as several lollipops or packs of sweets. A single can of cola equates to 35 g of sugar, the same as three-and-a-half lollipops or one-and-a-quarter packs of fruit sweets. And energy drinks can be even **worse**, with as much as 20 teaspoons of sugar in one can.

Many experts and parents are becoming **concerned** about the amount of sugar children are consuming, without even realising it. "Soft drinks aren't just a drink – they contain **frightening** amounts of hidden sugar," says one doctor.

There are far fewer water fountains available now, and a bottle of water often costs nearly as much as a soft drink. As a result, young people are tempted to buy a sugary soft drink, especially if it's promoted as containing health-giving vitamins or being energy boosting.

"Soft drinks are designed to be very appealing for children," says one mum, "And there is so much choice – all in neon colours and funky bottles and cans. Why would anyone choose water rather than some bright, appealing fruity, fizzy drink? They don't advertise their **threats** to health."

Some schools are now taking action to prevent children from having access to these drinks during the day. Head teacher Nabil Singh says: "We have removed all vending machines selling sugary snacks and drinks from our school and replaced them with healthier alternatives, despite protests from students. We have to put their health first. Some of these drinks are no better than sugary **poison**."

## Understanding

**Using the article, answer these questions.**

1. How much sugar can there be in an energy drink?
2. Give two reasons why young people buy soft drinks.
3. What is one school doing to reduce the amount of sugar young people consume?

4. Explain in your own words how you know some students in the school aren't happy about this decision.
5. What is the purpose of this text? Summarise this in one sentence.
6. Identify the text type of this extract. Explain your answer.

## Glossary

**neon** very bright in colour

**vending machines** machines that sell snacks and drinks

## Word builder

**Answer the following questions.**

1. Explain how each word in the Word cloud tries to create a negative impression of sugary drinks.
2. This article also contains positive language to show why sugary drinks are attractive to young people. Write down all the words from the article in the positive lexical field.

### Looking closely

When writers use a group of words to create a particular effect, it is called a lexical field. In Greek, *lexis* means 'word', and *lexikos* means 'of words'.

## Developing your language – paragraphs

**Answer the following questions.**

1. Look at the article on page 8 and write down the key idea in each paragraph.
2. Find two paragraphs in the article that start with a topic sentence. Write down the topic sentences.
3. Look at the first paragraph. Suggest why it is so short.
4. Write a short newspaper article, of no more than 300 words, with the following headline.

**Students protest as sugary drinks banned**

First, write a brief plan. Organise your ideas into three short paragraphs, using topic sentences.

5. When you have written your article, swap with a partner and check each other's sentences and paragraphs. Experiment by re-ordering your paragraphs – which order is the most effective?

### Remember

A topic sentence can be used at the beginning of each paragraph to introduce the main idea within it.

Key concept

## More spelling 'rules'

Here are some more 'rules' to help you with spelling. Note there also exceptions to these rules!

1. The letter 'q' is usually followed by 'u'. **Example**: quiet.
2. Put 'i' before 'e' except after 'c', when the sound is 'ee'. **Examples**: chief, deceive. **Exception**: seize.
3. The sound 'ee' at the end of a word is almost always spelt with a 'y'. **Example**: emergency. **Exceptions**: coffee, fee.
4. Words ending with the sound 'ick' are usually spelt 'ick' if they have one syllable. If they have more than one syllable, they end in 'ic'. **Examples**: brick, electronic. **Exceptions**: homesick, limerick.
5. When an ending that begins with a vowel is added to words that end in a silent 'e', the 'e' is dropped. **Example**: giving.
6. When 'all', 'well', 'full', and 'till' are preceded or followed by another syllable, one 'l' is dropped. **Examples**: already, welcome, helpful, until.

## Practising your spelling

**Complete the following activities.**

1. For each of the rules opposite, make a list of further examples.
2. There are also words which you just have to learn. For each word in the following list, check your spelling. A good method to do this is: look, say, cover, write, check.

| | | | | |
|---|---|---|---|---|
| accommodation | calendar | development | friends | separate |
| appearance | chocolate | disappoint | government | sincerely |
| argument | climb | embarrass | happened | successful |
| basically | completely | environment | imaginary | truly |
| beginning | concentration | existence | interesting | unfortunately |
| buried | conscious | familiar | interrupt | which |
| business | definitely | finally | knowledge | |

3. For three of the words above, invent fun ways of remembering their spellings. For example, you could use a mnemonic:

Necessary = **n**ever **e**at **c**ake, **e**at **s**alty **s**nacks **a**nd **r**emain **y**oung

Or you can draw a cartoon like this:

## Creating your own game

**In groups, discuss ideas of possible games you can play to improve your spelling.** Design your game with accompanying rules. Test this out with your group, making improvements as necessary before swapping your game with another group.

## Healthy eating – a radio discussion

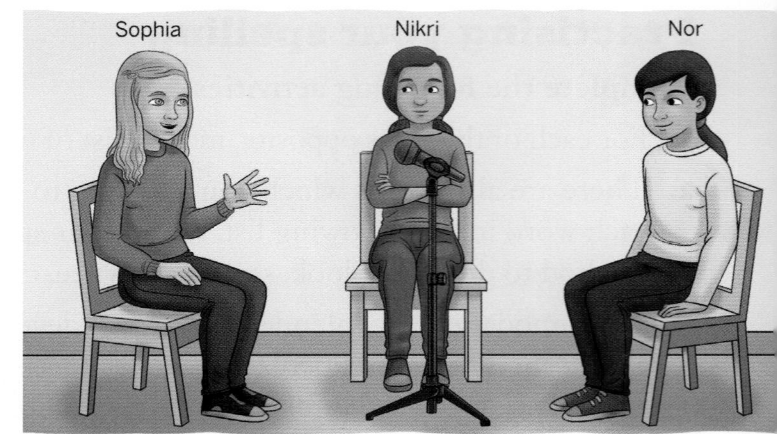


Sophia, Nikri, and Nor have been asked to discuss how young people can be encouraged to eat healthily.

**Listen carefully to their discussion.** Sophia starts the discussion.

### Understanding

**Answer the following questions.**

1. Sophia's and Nikri's mothers have the same view of food. What is it?
2. What do Nor, Sophia, and Nikri think young people need to eat to stay healthy?
3. What do they think are the foods you should eat less of?
4. a Give two ways the group suggest of persuading young people to eat healthily.
   b Which method do you think is more effective? Explain your answer.

### Looking closely

'Nutritious' and 'nutrients' come from the same word family. They both come from Latin: nutritious from *nutrex* (meaning nurse) and nutrients from *nutrire* (meaning to nourish).

## Word builder

The words in the Word cloud are all subject-specific words linked to the topic of nutrition and diet. **Look at the Word cloud and answer the following questions.**

1. Check you know what each word in the Word cloud means. Use a dictionary to help you.
2. Give some examples of foods in each category.
3. Add three other subject-specific words linked to this topic.

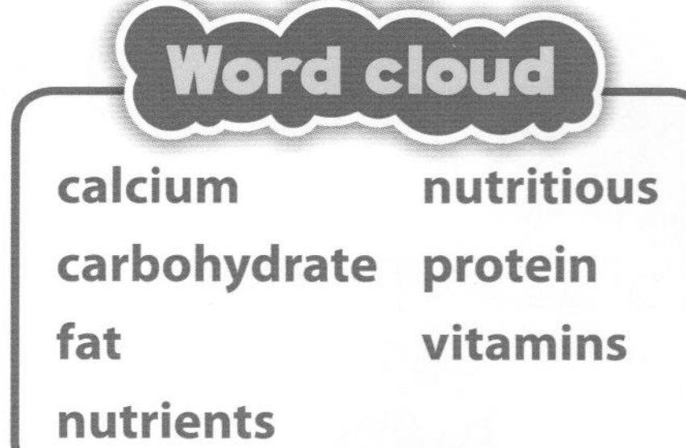

## Developing your language – writing appropriately for the reader

Sophia, Nikri, and Nor talk about *how* to convey information about healthy eating effectively for young people. **Answer the following questions about literary features.**

1. What do the group suggest as being important?

2. Look at the list of features below and decide which you think are important and which are not. Explain your answer.

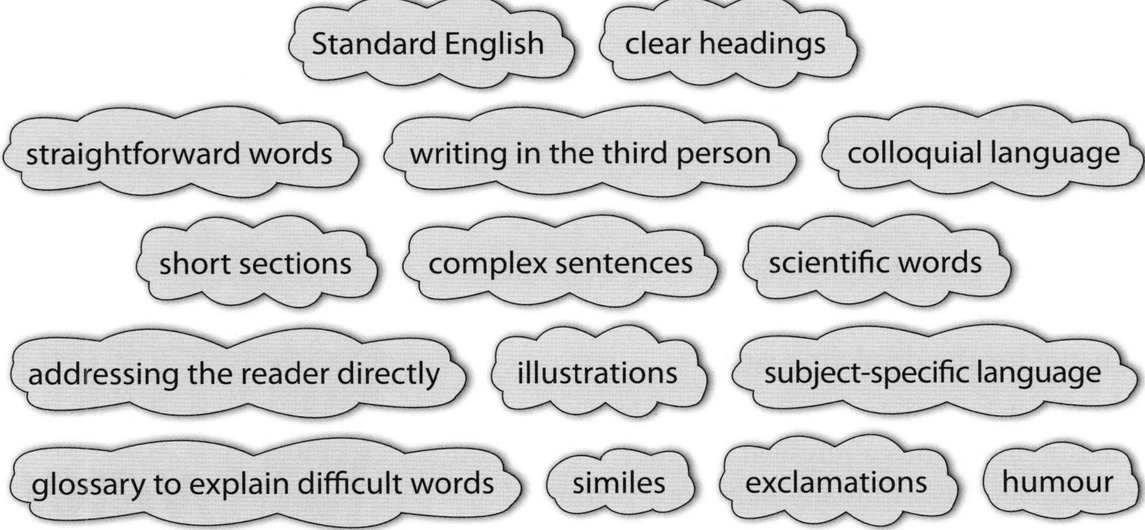


3. Add other ideas of features to the group above.
4. Using the information from the discussion, and your own knowledge, write an information leaflet for students of your age to encourage them to eat healthily.

   You need to think about:

   - what you are going to include in your leaflet
   - how to make your leaflet encouraging and persuasive for young people
   - how you are going to organise your ideas clearly.

## Your favourite foods

**Discuss your favourite foods in a group.** What are they, and why do you like them so much? Consider the following questions:

- What is your favourite food?
- What do you like about it?
- What nutritional value does this food have, if any?
- From a scientific perspective, could you live without this food?

## Promoting healthy eating

In this section you are going to design and promote a healthy snack or drink.

### Planning your product

First, you need to decide:

- what your drink or snack is going to be
- the ways in which it is healthy (you may need to do some research here)
- an appealing name for the drink or snack.

Use a big sheet of paper for your planning. If you can actually develop your drink or snack into a physical product, so that you can see it in front of you, this will really help your planning!

### Promoting your product

Once you have decided what your snack or drink is going to be, promote your snack in the following ways:

- Produce a letter for supermarkets, head teachers, or parents about your healthy snack or drink.
- Produce a TV advertisement for your healthy snack or drink.

### Writing your letter

A formal letter needs to have your address (use your school address) as well as the address of the person and/or company you are writing to. It should also include the date and the correct salutation and valediction (greeting and farewell).

Academy of Excellence
Port Road
Castletown

Ms R Brahmani
Manager
Superdeal Supermarket
Castletown
14 February

Dear Ms Brahmani,

**Remember**

If you begin a formal letter 'Dear Sir/Madam' you should end it 'Yours faithfully'. If you begin with a name, you should end 'Yours sincerely'.

### Planning

Plan your letter. Remember that, while the purpose of your letter will be the same, *how* you write your letter to a supermarket, head teacher, or parent will be slightly different.

When you plan, make sure you organise your ideas into paragraphs, using topic sentences where helpful.

### Writing

Write your letter to the intended audience. As you write, keep going back to your plan and remember to write in sentences and paragraphs. Every few sentences, stop writing and read what you have written so far, trying to hear it in your head, and checking that it is clear and makes sense.

### Editing

Go through your letter, checking it against your plan and making sure that you have included everything you need to include. Are there sections that need deleting? Adding? Amending?

### Proofreading

This is the final stage in the writing process where you make sure every detail is correct. The recipients will not take any notice of a letter that has punctuation or spelling errors.

Where possible, ask another person to check your letter for accuracy.

### Giving feedback

**Swap your letter with another student to give each other feedback.** Think about:

- how informative/persuasive the content of the letter is
- how well it is adapted to the particular audience
- how clearly and accurately it is written.

Give feedback on each of these points, and say how far you would be convinced by your partner's letter.

## Speaking and listening

**Devise a TV advertisement for your healthy drink or snack.**

Start by discussing what makes a good TV advertisement. Research TV advertisements by watching some at home and write down a list of the features they use.

Discuss your list with others, then write a script for your TV advertisement. Rehearse it and either perform your advertisement for the rest of the class or film it.

## Progress check

1. Suggest two of the problems caused by having too much choice. [2 marks]
2. Explain what a word family is. [1 mark]
3. Give examples of three words from the same word family. [3 marks]
4. Write an explanation of what a sentence is. [1 mark]
5. Write one simple, one compound, and one complex sentence. [3 marks]
6. How can you tell that commas are being used to mark a parenthetical phrase? [1 mark]
7. What is a lexical field? Give an example of a lexical field and suggest three words belonging to it. [2 marks]
8. What does a topic sentence do? Give an example of a topic sentence. [2 marks]
9. Write down two spelling rules. Give two examples of words that follow each spelling rule. [4 marks]
10. Give one way of remembering how to spell a difficult word of your choice. [1 mark]
11. How should you end letters that begin in the following ways?
    - **a** Dear Sir/Madam
    - **b** Dear Mrs Azizi [2 marks]
12. Give four literary features found in a persuasive piece of writing. For each feature, give an explanation and an example. [8 marks]

## Reflecting on your learning

How confident do you feel about different features used in writing? Here is a quick checklist. **Decide how confident you feel about each of these skills.**

| | Very confident | Quite confident | Not very confident |
|---|---|---|---|
| I know what a sentence is. | | | |
| I know how to punctuate a sentence. | | | |
| I can use commas to mark parenthetical phrases. | | | |
| I know what paragraphs are. | | | |
| I know what a topic sentence is. | | | |
| I can use paragraphs in my own writing. | | | |
| I know the format of a formal letter. | | | |
| I know ways of learning and remembering spellings. | | | |
| I can listen carefully to people talking. | | | |
| I can work successfully in a group. | | | |
| I can express my ideas in front of my fellow students. | | | |
| I can read and understand texts. | | | |
| I can recognise the features of a newspaper article. | | | |
| I know what a lexical field is. | | | |

**Write a short paragraph explaining what you feel confident about, and which skills you need to develop further in the future.** Make suggestions of how you can improve these skills.

# 2 Amazing arts

**In this unit you will:**

**Explore**
- the use of bias and its effects
- the strange world of a Dickens novel

**Create**
- your own drama script
- your own collection of synonyms and antonyms

**Engage**
- with reading pre-twentieth century literature
- with how memorable characters are created

**Collaborate**
- in a problem solving exercise
- to bounce ideas around

**Reflect**
- on the worldwide appeal of Shakespeare's plays
- on how writers from the past are still relevant today

Miranda and Prospero watch the storm in Shakespeare's *The Tempest*

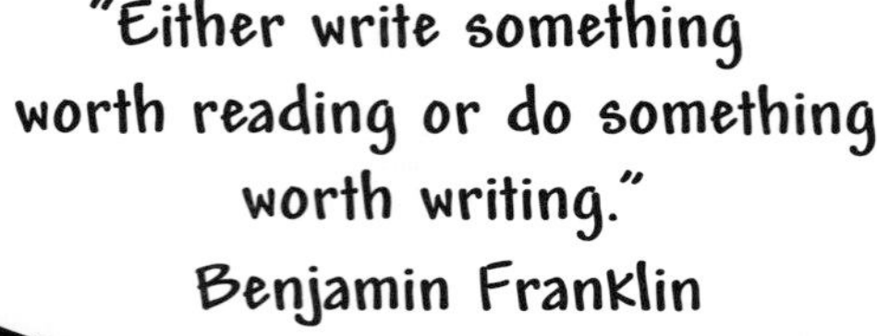


'A brave vessel who had, no doubt, some noble creature in her, dashed all to pieces.'
William Shakespeare, The Tempest

I only enjoy reading a story when I am interested in what happens to the characters.

## Thinking time

*The Tempest* by William Shakespeare is a play that begins with a great storm but ends happily for those characters who are honest and good.

1. What will happen to a small wooden ship caught in a huge violent storm?
2. Why do you think a storm is an effective way to begin a story or play?
3. What qualities must a story have for you to want to read it?
4. Does a story have to end happily for the main characters to make it enjoyable?
5. Do you think it is important for a story to have a moral?

## Speaking and listening – problem solving

You are travelling on a ship that is caught in a terrible storm and sinks. While escaping, you only have time to collect five items from the list in the box opposite. You manage to reach safety on a deserted island.

**Complete the following activity.**

1. Discuss which five items you would choose, bearing in mind your survival depends on them.
2. Create a table like the one below. Fill it in while you are having your discussion.

| COLLECT | | LEAVE BEHIND | |
|---|---|---|---|
| Item | Reason | Item | Reason |
| | | | |

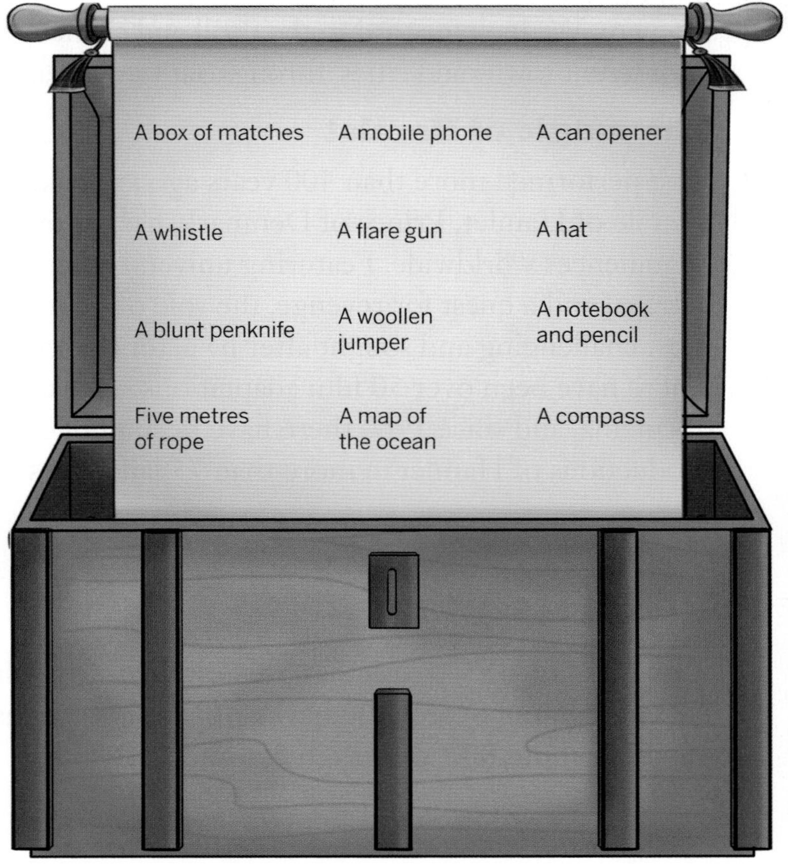

## The world's most famous play

### Hamlet in the round (and about town)

'Hamlet in the round (and about town)' is an **extraordinary** modern interpretation of William Shakespeare's most **iconic** play, in all its **multifarious** glory. Here in Market Newtown, our very own Newtown Players have recreated the court intrigue of Elsinore with a **unique** twist. Inspired by open-air theatre but on an **unprecedented** scale, each performance takes place in a variety of locations across town. Taking in the parks, town square and ruins of the old castle, this **incredible** production makes the most of the local scenery, changing locations between acts and performing some scenes while on the move.

The production has already received acclaim in the national press, as well as on television, and has been nominated for several **prestigious** theatre awards. The cast of top graduates from our **renowned** theatre school has received particular praise for its energy and freshness of approach. According to Artistic Director Rupert Cartwright, "The next step is to obtain funding to take the show on the road, and that's looking really promising at the moment. We look forward to the thrill and challenge of performing in different towns and cities, throughout the UK and beyond."

### The magic of Hamlet

First performed more than 400 years ago at Shakespeare's Globe, the tale of Hamlet, Prince of Denmark, has captivated generations of audiences worldwide. Featuring universal themes of murder, betrayal and a quest for revenge, the role of Hamlet is one of the most challenging and sought after by actors of stage and film. There have been over 50 film adaptations since the invention of cinema, and since 1960 there have been publications and productions of Hamlet in more than 75 languages.

### Word cloud

extraordinary
iconic
incredible
multifarious
prestigious
renowned
unique
unprecedented

### Glossary

**Artistic Director** the person who decides how, what, and where a theatre company performs

**Elsinore** a city in Denmark which is the setting for much of *Hamlet*

**in the round** a centred stage with the audience arranged on at least three sides

**Shakespeare's Globe** the Globe Theatre in London

**take the show on the road** go on tour to other destinations

## Understanding

*Hamlet* is one of 37 plays that Shakespeare wrote during his life. He contributed over 2,000 new words to the English language, of which about 800 are still in common use today.

**Answer the following questions.**

1. How does this version of Hamlet claim to be different from others that have come before it?
2. What examples in the text indicate that 'Hamlet in the round' has been well-received?
3. What evidence is there to suggest Shakespeare's stories appeal to a worldwide audience?
4. What difficulties might audiences in other countries face when watching the translated plays of Shakespeare?

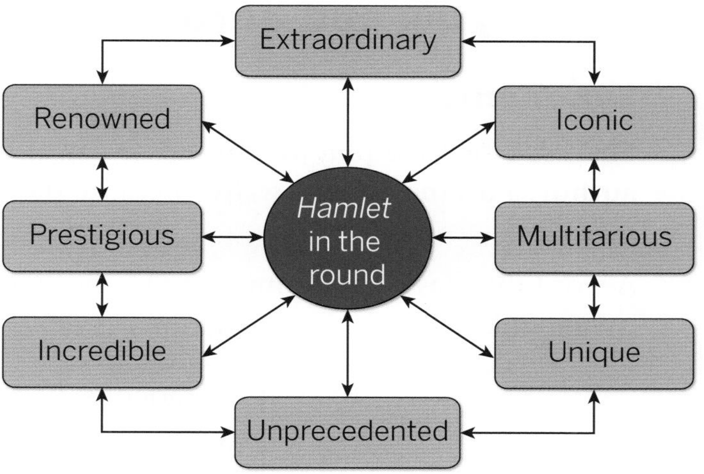


## Developing your language – creating bias

Many writers create a bias in their writing. Read this extract from an alternative review of the 'Hamlet in the round (and about town)' tour. The words in bold all suggest a negative bias in the review.

'I recently read about this misguided theatre company that foolishly wants to perform Shakespeare's 'Hamlet' not on stage but across multiple outdoor locations! Why? Why would a group of talented actors ever consider such a fool's errand? In my opinion, 'Hamlet' is one of Shakespeare's most difficult plays to understand. In addition, the average length of a production is around four hours! And that doesn't include walking all over town! A slow burner, some may say, or is it just painfully tedious? And the language! Not only is it written in a language which is obsolete, but most of it is in a redundant poetic style far removed from the way we speak today. A noble but flawed vision, I'm afraid; much like the character of Hamlet himself.'

### Glossary

**flawed** containing some error or fault

**fool's errand** a task that has no hope of success

**obsolete** out of date; no longer in use

**redundant** no longer needed or useful

**slow burner** something that is not immediately impressive but becomes so with time

**Answer the following questions.**

1. Pick out the other words and phrases that are used to create the negative bias.
2. How does the reviewer's use of question marks and exclamation marks add to the negative impression?

## Word builder

Look at the Word cloud on page 20. All eight words are adjectives chosen to impress on the reader the special nature of the performance.

If you have a thesaurus, create your own range of positive adjectives based on the words in the Word cloud.

## Synonyms and antonyms

### Synonyms

Shakespeare was a **playwright** but he can also be described as an **author**, a **dramatist** or a **writer** because the words have similar meanings.

A word that has a *similar* meaning to another word is called a 'synonym'. A hero is often described as brave.

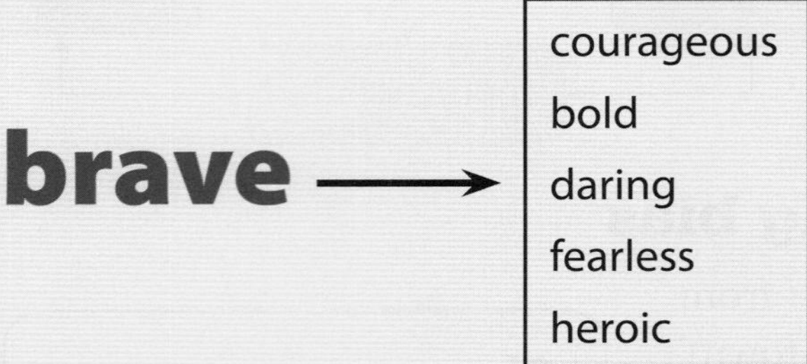


He can also be described as shy.

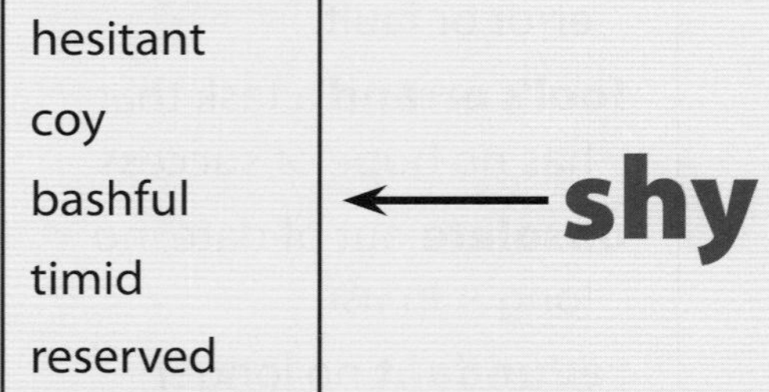


The famous balcony scene from *Romeo and Juliet*

**Answer the questions.**

1. Create your own list of synonyms for each of these heroic qualities.

   **a** innocent **b** proud

   **c** honest **d** faithful

2. Use an alternative synonym for each word in bold in the following passage.

   *Romeo and Juliet* is a **play** by Shakespeare about two **important** families who **hate** each other because of an **ancient argument**. Romeo is the **handsome** son of the Montagues who falls in love with Juliet, the **beautiful** only daughter of the Capulets. The families **fight** each other but in the end become **friends**. The play is set in the **busy** city of Verona.

3. Choose a word expressing emotion such as *happy* or *sad*. How many synonyms can you think of for it?

## Antonyms

An 'antonym' is a word that is the *opposite* of another word:

- ***question*** is an antonym for ***answer***
- ***war*** is an antonym for ***peace.***

Antonyms do not have to be nouns:

| | Antonyms | |
|---|---|---|
| Verbs | ***love*** | ***hate*** |
| Adverbs | ***inside*** | ***outside*** |
| Adjectives | ***good*** | ***bad*** |
| Prepositions | ***to*** | ***from*** |

Antonyms are really useful when juxtaposing different ideas.

**Answer the following questions.**

**1.** Copy and complete the table by adding antonyms.

| HERO | VILLAIN |
|---|---|
| | cowardly |
| honest | |
| trustworthy | |
| | immoral |
| gentle | |
| loyal | |
| | ugly |
| innocent | |

Language is complicated, so sometimes the opposites are not as clearly definable as they initially appear.

Take **day** and **night**, for example. These are antonyms, but each can be described in a number of ways.

**2.** Write two lists – one for all the nouns to describe 'day' and one for 'night'. Use the example below as your starting point.

| Day | Night |
|---|---|
| morning | midnight |

**Key concept**

### Synonyms and antonyms

Synonyms and antonyms can be used to add variation and depth to your writing.

Synonyms have similar meanings but there are subtle differences, as two words rarely have exactly the same meaning.

Antonyms are opposites but there can still be subtle variations in meaning.

## Great Expectations

### Miss Havisham

Pip, a young boy, has been sent to visit Miss Havisham at Satis House. He is surprised and shocked by what he finds.

confusedly heaped
scattered
shrunk
sunken
withered

In an armchair, with an elbow resting on a table and her head leaning on her hand, sat the strangest lady I have ever seen ...

She was dressed in rich materials, satins, and lace, and silks – all of white. Her shoes were white. And she had a long white veil dependent from her hair, and she had bridal flowers in her hair, but her hair was white. Some bright jewels sparkled on her neck and on her hands, and some other jewels lay sparkling on the table. Dresses, less splendid than the dress she wore, and half-packed trunks, were **scattered** about. She had not quite finished dressing, for she had but one shoe on – the other was on the table near her hand – her veil was but half arranged, her watch and chain were not put on, and some lace for her bosom lay with those trinkets, and with her handkerchief, and gloves, and some flowers, and a prayer-book, all **confusedly heaped** about the looking-glass.

It was not in the first few moments that I saw these things, though I saw more of them in the first few moments than might be supposed. But, I saw that everything within my view which ought to be white, had been white long ago, and had lost its lustre, and was faded and yellow. I saw that the bride within the bridal dress had **withered** like the dress, and like the flowers, and had no brightness left but the brightness of her **sunken** eyes. I saw that the dress had been put upon the rounded figure of a young woman, and that the figure on which it now hung loose, had **shrunk** to skin and bone.

From *Great Expectations* by Charles Dickens

### Glossary

**looking-glass** mirror

**lost its lustre** no longer bright and shiny

**Miss Havisham** a woman abandoned by her fiancé on their wedding day

**satins, and lace, and silks** expensive materials

**those trinkets** items of jewellery

**skin and bone** painfully thin

## Understanding

**Answer the following questions.**

1. What does the narrator think about Miss Havisham?
2. Why might her appearance frighten a child?
3. What is the significance of Miss Havisham still being dressed in the clothes she wore on her wedding day?
4. How effective is Dickens' description of Miss Havisham?

## Developing your language – creating a character

Dickens is famous for his memorable characters. Miss Havisham is a particularly fine example. He uses several techniques.

***Pathos is an appeal to the emotions of the audience. Here it is used to create a feeling of pity and sympathy for Miss Havisham***

'I saw that the dress had been put upon the rounded figure of a young woman, and that the figure on which it now hung loose, had shrunk to skin and bone.'

***'She had not quite finished dressing, for she had but one shoe on – the other was on the table near her hand.'***

Observed detail – Pip narrates everything he sees in minute detail, giving the reader an exact impression of what has become of Miss Havisham.

Below are more techniques. Find quotations to illustrate them.

1. Shades of white are used to contrast how Miss Havisham was on her wedding day and how she has decayed.
2. There is a sense of time having passed.
3. First person narrative – we see Miss Havisham through the eyes of an intelligent but frightened young boy.

## Word builder

Dickens has chosen his vocabulary very carefully to exaggerate how strange and frightening Miss Havisham looks to Pip.

**Answer the following questions.**

1. Miss Havisham's clothes and possessions are 'confusedly heaped' and 'scattered' in the room. Which of the following could have been used in the same context?

   neatly ordered    flung haphazardly    thrown
   placed carefully    abandoned

2. Miss Havisham is described as having physically 'withered' and 'shrunk'. If Dickens had used a simile, which of these might he have likened her to?

   a dying leaf    a healthy tree
   a rotting piece of fruit    a deflated balloon

## Semi-colons

A semi-colon looks like a comma with a full stop on top of it; it signals a stronger break than a comma, but it is not as final as the break provided by a full stop.

Semi-colons are used in three ways.

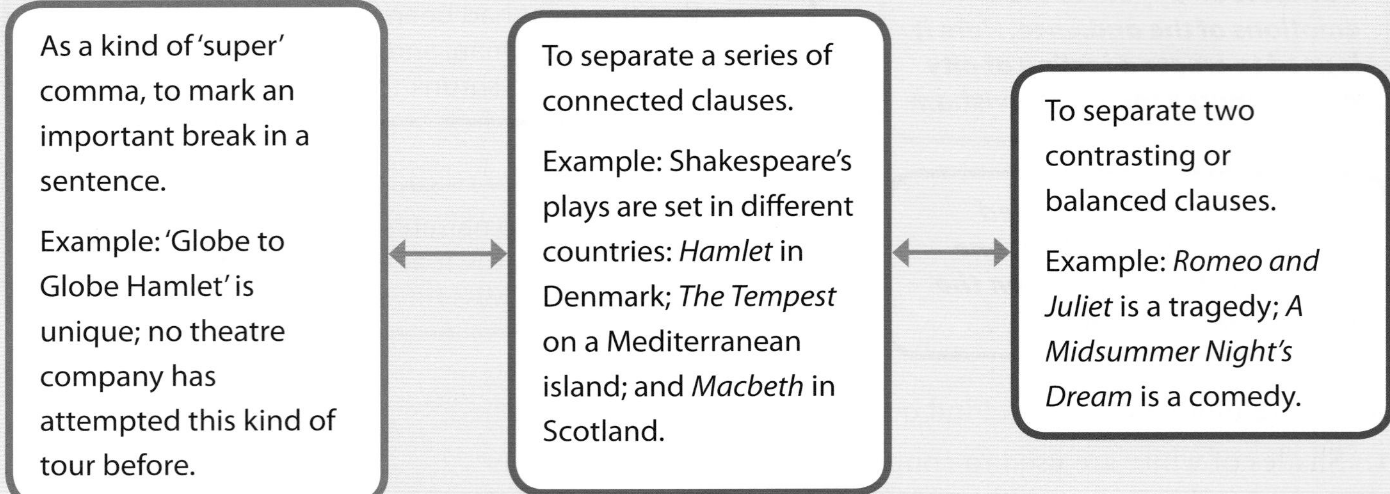


**Place the semi-colon in the correct position in these sentences.**

1. My best friend loves Shakespeare I prefer Dickens.
2. A study of 100 teenagers revealed the following results: 30% enjoyed watching Shakespeare 20% agreed to liking the storylines but not following the language 36% found the plots complicated and difficult to follow and 14% admitted to being unable to access the language at all.
3. In my opinion *Great Expectations* is the best Dickens novel because of the interesting characters *A Tale of Two Cities* is his worst because the plot is so weak.
4. The main speakers at the recent Shakespeare convention were: Professor James Underwood, Cambridge University Neesha Patel, author and journalist Diego Montalban, actor and Giles Simmons, Royal Shakespeare Company.

## Using semi-colons for description

Dickens made considerable use of semi-colons in his writing, particularly when he was describing a character or location.

Ours was the marsh country, down by the river, within, as the river wound, twenty miles of the sea. My first most vivid and broad impression of the identity of things, seems to me to have been gained on a memorable raw afternoon towards evening. At such a time I found out for certain, that this bleak place overgrown with nettles was the churchyard; and that Philip Pirrip, late of this parish, and also Georgiana wife of the above, were dead and buried; and that Alexander, Bartholomew, Abraham, Tobias and Roger, infant children of the aforesaid, were also dead and buried; and that the dark flat wilderness beyond the churchyard, intersected with dykes and mounds and gates, with scattered cattle feeding on it, was the marshes; and that the low leaden line beyond, was the river; and that the distant savage lair from which the wind was rushing was the sea; and that the small bundle of shivers growing afraid of it all and beginning to cry, was Pip.

From *Great Expectations* by Charles Dickens

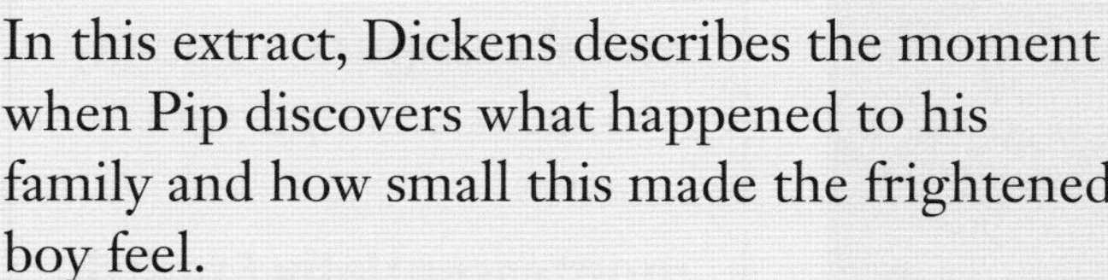

In this extract, Dickens describes the moment when Pip discovers what happened to his family and how small this made the frightened boy feel.

Think about the clauses separated by the semi-colons as concentric circles to illustrate Dickens's technique.

**Complete the following activity.**

1. Think about your own life. Draw your own version of the circles, beginning with you at the centre and expanding outwards.
2. Now turn your drawing into a sentence using semi-colons to separate your clauses.

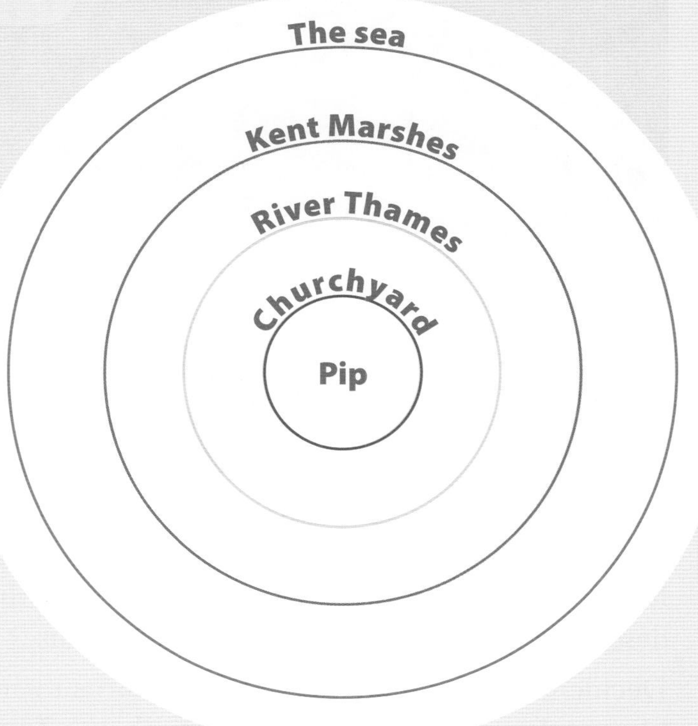

## 'Great Expectations – The Play'

Listen to a fictional interview with artistic director Boz Charles, conducted by Mei Chun, the arts presenter at a television studio.

## Understanding

A touring theatre company will often seek promotion of its show through interaction with the local media.

**Answer these questions.**

1. In which city is the interview taking place?
2. What is Mei Chun's favourite part of *Great Expectations?*
3. Summarise the reasons for Boz Charles being inspired to choose a Dickens novel as a subject.
4. How might the themes of *Great Expectations* still be relevant today?
5. What difficulties might there be in adapting a novel to a play?

## Speaking and listening – similes game

Boz Charles uses a simile that describes Pip 'like a rabbit in the headlights' to show how scared he was on seeing Miss Havisham for the first time. What other similes can you think of to describe Pip, Miss Havisham, and Satis House?

Decide who goes first, then take it in turns to create a simile. Give each other marks out of five for how effective you think each simile is.

### Word cloud

enduring
intimidated
overawed
perpetual
redundant
traumatised
unrequited
vicious

### Glossary

**caricatures** heavily exaggerated characters

**the Dickensian world** life as shown in the novels of Charles Dickens

**in modern parlance** in today's language

**like a rabbit in the headlights** a simile meaning frozen with fear

**moral compass** his ability to focus on important issues

**quintessentially English** stereotypically English in nature and style

**Satis House** Miss Havisham's home

**secret benefactor** unknown sponsor

## Word builder – creating atmosphere

Look at the Word cloud. The last six words are adjectives that describe a negative state, but they do so in varying ways.

**Now answer these questions.**

1. How does using ‘intimidated’, ‘overawed’ and ‘traumatised’ help to create sympathy for Pip?
2. Miss Havisham is described as being ‘vicious’. In this case there is no sympathy created for the character. In what ways does ‘vicious’ have different negative connotations from the other words in the Word cloud?
3. During the novel, Pip falls in love with Estella and decides he wants to marry her, but his love is ‘unrequited’ because Miss Havisham has raised Estella to be heartless and incapable of love. How does the use of ‘unrequited’ add to the negative atmosphere surrounding Pip?
4. Mei Chun suggests Dickens’ novel may be ‘redundant’ in today’s society because it is outdated and out of place in the contemporary world. How might the word also be appropriate to describe Miss Havisham?

## Developing your language – atmosphere through setting

Through the eyes of Pip, the reader is taken on a personal journey through Satis House that helps to build the feeling of a once important home now left to decay.

| **Before the wedding day:** | **When Pip visits:** |
|---|---|
| magnificent<br>welcoming | dilapidated<br>filthy |

1. Can you think of five or more words to add to each box?
2. Choose one of the completed boxes and use it as the basis for your own description of Satis House.

## Writing a dramatic scene

Re-read the extract from *Great Expectations* by Charles Dickens on page 24.

Many novels have been transformed into play scripts. You are going to adapt this extract into a drama scene.

### Preparation

First, you will need to research your characters. One way is to use a character map like the one below.

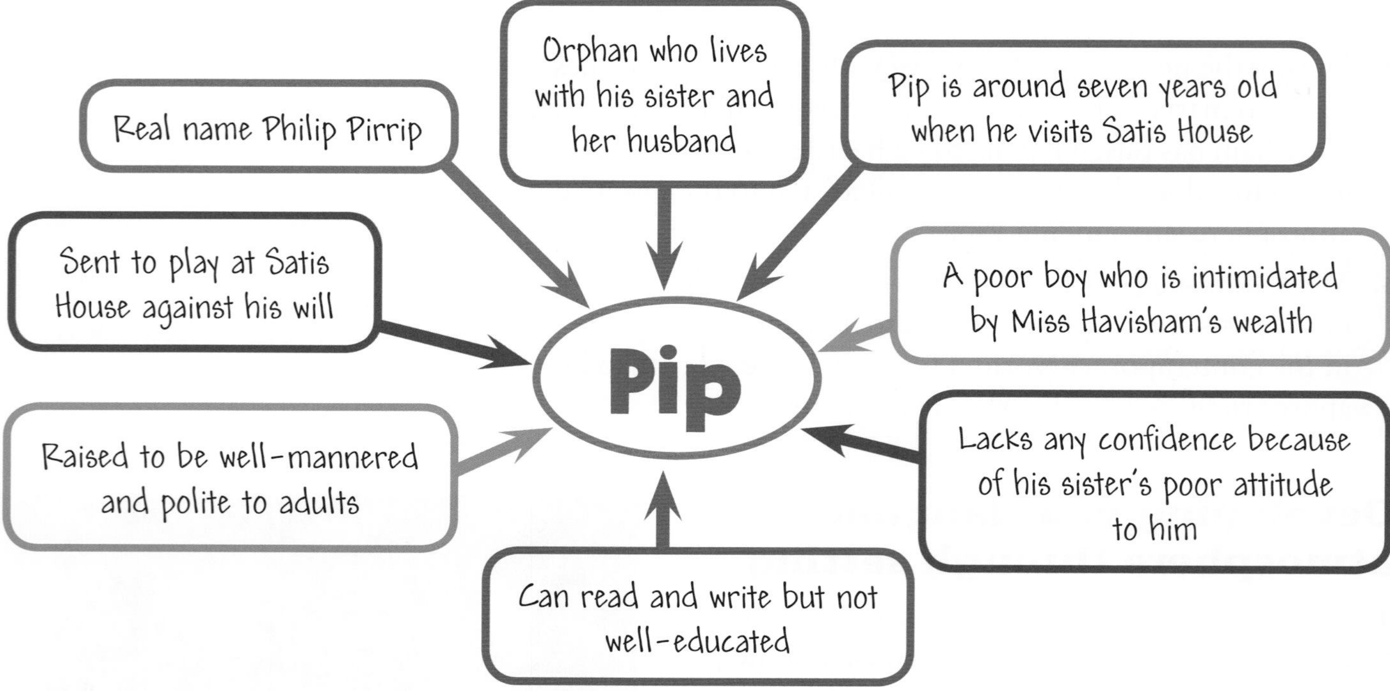


**Now complete the following activity.**

1. Write your own character map for Miss Havisham.
2. Once you have more understanding of the characters, you can begin to map how each will behave in the scene. To do so, add to the boxes below.

| **Pip** | **Miss Havisham** |
|---|---|
| frightened – young and inexperienced | bitter – wants revenge on all males |
| intimidated – in a strange place | powerful – wealthy and in control |

You can use these boxes as a guide when planning the conversation between Pip and Miss Havisham for the writing activity on the next page.

## Setting the scene

Drama scripts are set out differently from works of prose. To adapt the scene, you need to take into account the differences.

*Great Expectations* – the prose novel

- direct link between the writer and the reader
- first person narrative seen from Pip's perspective
- detailed description of the characters
- everything is experienced through reading and imagining the scene
- Dickens uses a whole page to describe what Pip sees and how he feels

*Great Expectations* – a drama script

- no direct link between the writer and the audience
- the audience experiences everything by watching the actions of the characters and listening to their dialogue
- stage directions guide the actors' performances
- the audience **sees** the physical scene and **interprets** the emotions through the actors' performances

Stage directions need to be precise, helpful to the actors and brief:

**Havisham:** (coldly) Well what is it boy? Haven't you seen an old woman before?

**Pip:** (politely but trembling with fear) Excuse me ma'am, I am new to all this and have no intention to cause offence.

## Speaking and listening – bouncing ideas

1. Write the opening stage directions for the scene. Allow your partner to read them.
2. Now draw a rough sketch of how the scene looks.
3. Your partner then describes the opening scene, using the sketch.
4. Discuss whether this description matches how you imagined the scene to be.
5. If necessary, revise your written version of the opening stage directions.

**Write your scene, using the skills you have learnt.**

## Looking closely

The opening stage directions may be more detailed, to include:

- a description of the room and its contents
- a description of the characters and where they are situated
- the kind of lighting to be used to create atmosphere.

## Progress check

1. Give two reasons why starting a story with a major event such as a shipwreck is a good idea. [2 marks]
2. If stranded on a desert island, which item would you choose to save and why: a length of rope or a blunt penknife? [2 marks]
3. Explain the meaning of the title, 'Hamlet in the round (and about town)'. [2 marks]
4. What do 'brave' and 'courageous' have in common, and can you add a third word to the list? [2 marks]
5. In what form of writing would you use a stage direction and for what purpose? [2 marks]
6. What is an antonym and when might you use one? Give two antonyms for 'brave'. [4 marks]
7. 'Shakespeare is a fantastic playwright who tells amazing stories.' Which two words used in this sentence suggest the writer is biased? Substitute the words with less complimentary alternatives to change the bias. [4 marks]
8. Give four examples of why Pip found Miss Havisham and her house so strange. [4 marks]
9. Name two reasons why a semi-colon might be used and give an example for each. [4 marks]
10. State four differences between a novel and a play. [4 marks]

## Reflecting on your learning

"All the world's a stage, and all the men and women merely players."
– *William Shakespeare*

Consider your progress through this unit to be similar to performing in a play. Assessing your experience as accurately as you can, which stage best reflects your performance?

I needed a lot of encouragement to go on stage at all.

I was not very confident and needed help with my performance from the other actors and the director.

My performance was solid but I know I could do better with more practice.

My performance was good and well-received, but not perfect.

My performance was near perfect. I was the star of the show.

### My action plan: preparing for the next performance

1. What do I need to do next to improve my performance?
2. Which of these script writing skills did I struggle with?
   - Using stage directions effectively
   - Setting out the script on the page
   - Understanding how my characters should behave and what they should say
   - Knowing how to end the scene

# 3 Terrific technology

In this unit you will:

**Explore**
- the use of genetically modified (GM) crops worldwide
- the use of robots on a future Earth

**Create**
- rhetorical questions
- a speech on the subject of artificial intelligence (AI)

**Engage**
- with the arguments for and against artificial intelligence
- with the issues surrounding GM crops

**Collaborate**
- in a constructive argument
- in a hot seating exercise

**Reflect**
- on the human reaction to advances in technology
- on whether science is a force for good or bad

Whenever scientists break new ground someone panics.

A man who speaks a thousand words doesn't always say much at all.

Lots of people are good at speaking but far fewer people know how to listen.

## Thinking time

People sometimes object to scientific and technological progress. Look at the photographs and read the quotes.

1. What are the people doing in the two photographs?
2. How can you speak 'a thousand words' and not say much?
3. Why do you think listening is an important skill to master?
4. In what ways do you think people might feel threatened by scientific and technological progress?

## Speaking and listening – making your point

1. You are going to engage in a constructive argument. Here are the rules:

   No insults. No shouting. Don't interrupt. Listen carefully.

   a Consider this question: 'What is your favourite piece of technology?'

   b List five reasons to support your opinion.

   c Present your reasons and listen carefully to others as they present the reasons for their choices.

   d Now choose a partner to debate with.

2. It is important to reflect on the strengths and weaknesses of your contribution to a constructive argument. Use the scale below, where 1 is the lowest and 10 is the highest.

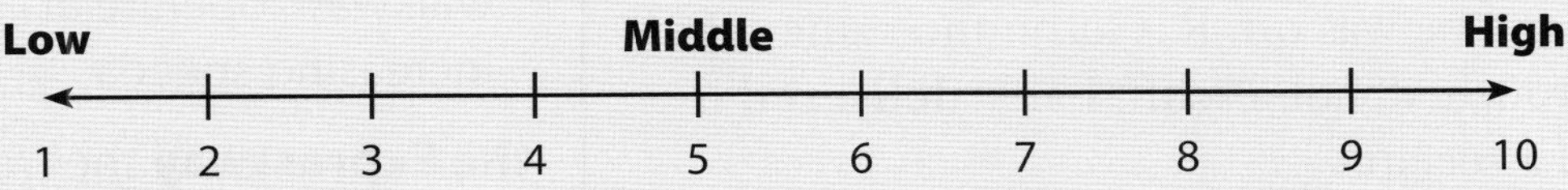


   a How strong (convincing) were the points you made?

   b How good were you at listening to your partner's argument?

   c How do you rate your overall performance?

3. Now, using the same scale and the same questions, rate your partner's performance.
4. Compare and discuss your results.

# The Robots of Dawn

He heard the teenage cry of 'Robot!' (he had been a teenager himself once) and knew exactly what would happen. A group of them—two or three or half a dozen—would swarm up or down the strips and somehow the robot would be tripped and would go clanging down. Then, if it ever came before a magistrate, any teenager taken into custody would claim the robot had **collided** with him and was a menace on the strips – and would undoubtedly be let go.

The robot could neither defend itself in the first instance, nor testify in the second.

Baley moved rapidly and was between the first of the teenagers and the robot. He sidestepped on to a faster strip, brought his arm higher, as though to adjust to the increase in wind speed, and somehow the young man was **nudged** off course and on to a slower strip for which he was not prepared. He called out wildly, 'Hey!' as he went sprawling. The others stopped, **assessed** the situation quickly, and **veered** away.

Baley said, 'On to the Expressway, boy.'

The robot **hesitated** briefly. Robots were not allowed, unaccompanied, on the Expressway. Baley's order had been a firm one, however, and it moved aboard. Baley followed, which relieved the pressure on the robot.

Baley moved brusquely through the crowd of standees, forcing R. Geronimo ahead of him, making his way up to the less crowded upper level. He held on to a pole and kept one foot firmly on the robot's, again glaring down all eye contact.

Fifteen and a half kilometres brought him to the close-point for the Police Headquarters and he was off. R. Geronimo came off with him. It hadn't been touched, not a scuff. Baley **delivered** it at the door and **accepted** a receipt.

From *The Robots of Dawn*, by Isaac Asimov

### Word cloud

accepted
assessed
collided
delivered
hesitated
nudged
veered

### Glossary

**the strips** a series of tiered moving walkways

**a menace on the strips** a danger to other users of the walkways

**a faster strip** the walkways operate at increasing speeds

**the Expressway** the fastest moving walkway

**Baley** the main character and a police inspector

**R. Geronimo** the robot's name (R signifying robot)

**close-point** an exit place

## Understanding

1. What are Baley and the robot travelling on?
2. How does Baley protect the robot from danger?

3. Why do you think the other teenagers moved away?
4. How does the incident show the two differing views humans have about robots at this time?
5. Do you share the teenagers' dislike of robots? If so, why?

## Writing a brief sales brochure

Consider how robots are used to do tasks that people normally do.

You are going to produce a brochure *selling* your robot. In your brochure, make sure you have:

- given your robot a name
- explained which tasks it can do (and which it cannot perform)
- stated the life expectancy of the robot
- covered any potential problem areas
- included a range of different ability levels, at different prices.

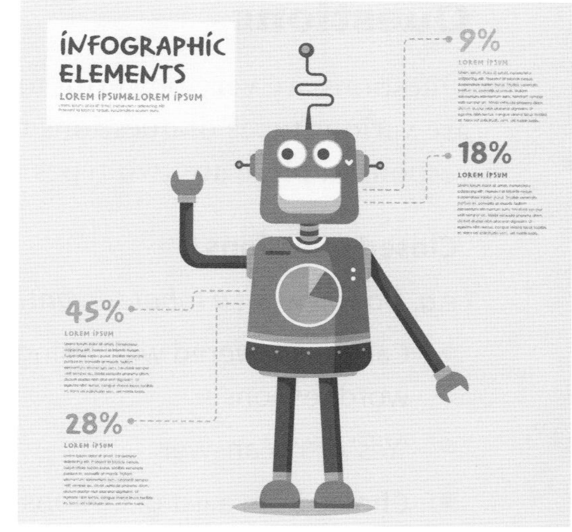


## Developing your language – regular and irregular verbs

Regular verbs follow conventional rules when conjugated.

Here, the focus is on tense. Asimov uses the **regular** verb *swarm*.

| Present tense | Past tense | Future tense |
|---|---|---|
| swarm | swarmed | will swarm |

The **irregular** verb *speak* doesn't follow conventional rules.

| Present tense | Past tense | Future tense |
|---|---|---|
| speak | spoke | will speak |

It would be incorrect to say: '***I speaked** to my friend last week.*'

1. Decide which of these verbs are **regular** and which are **irregular** by working out their conjugated forms.

come trip drink walk know hear stop bring testify

2. Conjugate each one using a table like the one above.

**Key concept**

**Regular and irregular verbs**

Regular verbs follow the rules when conjugated (e.g. by adding -ed to form the past tense), but irregular verbs do not follow a consistent pattern. You just have to learn what form they take.

**Remember**

Conjugate means to change the tense or subject of a verb.

## Word builder

Look at the Word cloud. What kind of words are they? Give two other tenses for each.

## Questions

Questions are very powerful tools when used properly. There are various types of questions that can be used to create different responses. Here are two types for you to think about:

**Closed questions**

*e.g. Do you want a robot servant?*

- Can be answered with a single-word response
- 'Yes' or 'no' answer
- Choice from a list of options
- Identifies a piece of information

**Open questions**

*e.g. What do you think of robots as servants?*

- Cannot be answered with a single-word response
- Requires a more thoughtful answer than 'yes' or 'no', i.e. a longer, more detailed response

### Phrasing a question

How you phrase a question will depend on what type it is. **Closed** questions are phrased differently from **open** questions.

**1.** **Closed** questions often begin:

Do you… Would you… Can you… Did you…
What… Who… When... Where… Are you…

Complete the closed question by adding a beginning from the box. The first one is done for you.

**a** Do you like robots?
**b** ______ is its name?
**c** ______ afford a robot?
**d** ______ satisfied with your robot?
**e** ______ did you first see the robot?
**f** ______ is in charge?
**g** ______ will it be ready to collect?
**h** ______ find the 'on' button?
**i** ______ buy that robot?

**2.** **Open** questions often begin:

What… Why… How…

Match the incomplete questions to the beginnings in the box.

**a** ........... can robots benefit society?
**b** ........... might robots be considered a threat to humans?
**c** ........... could happen if robots become too intelligent in the future?
**d** ........... potential advances are there likely to be in the field of robotics in the next ten years?

Here are two more types of questions that you hear often.

**Leading questions**

*e.g. Why are robot servants bad for humans?*

- Leads the answer by the use of the word 'bad'
- Robots are 'bad' so the question is 'why' not 'if'
- Suggests the responder's answer will agree with the question

**Rhetorical questions**

*e.g. Who wouldn't want a robot servant?*

- Doesn't really require an answer
- It assumes everyone would want a robot
- Makes the responder think about the idea
- Often used in speeches to connect with the audience

1. Decide which of these are leading questions and which are rhetorical.
   - **a** Artificial intelligence is always a good thing, isn't it?
   - **b** Is there any doubt that robots will continue to become more advanced?
   - **c** Can you think of a reason why robots help humanity to progress?
   - **d** Why do robots that look like humans scare people?
   - **e** Surely without technological advancement humankind would suffer?

2. Pick out the different kinds of questions used in this extract from a speech about A.I.

   'Isn't it wonderful that we no longer have to do boring, tedious tasks? Can you think back to what it was like before we invented A.I.? You couldn't complete half the tasks you can now, could you? And what about the dangers involved? Weren't miners, oil workers and construction workers all at risk? Now we have robots to do all those tasks isn't it easier? Whoever thinks A.I is a danger surely can't understand the benefits, can they? Isn't it just trouble-makers causing unrest for no reason?'

   - **a** What is the viewpoint expressed by the writer through the use of these questions?
   - **b** How successful is it?
   - **c** What kind of question is the fourth question?

**Key concept**

### Types of question

**Leading** questions, sometimes called ***loaded*** questions, *suggest* to the responder a viewpoint that should be taken. **Rhetorical** questions have the answer phrased in the question so there is no doubt what viewpoint is to be taken.

## A balanced argument

### The impact of biotechnology

Similar to the debate on the socio-economic impacts of genetically modified (GM) crops adoption, there are different opinions about the potential risks of the **cultivation** of GM crops for the environment and, in particular, **biodiversity**. While some judge the environmental risks of GM adoption as severe, others argue that the benefits of GM crops compared to conventional crops prevail and the risks are rather limited.

An often quoted and more recent study based on a literature review on the environmental impacts of GM crops with particular emphasis on biodiversity came to the conclusion that 'by increasing **yields**, decreasing **insecticide** use, increasing the use of more environmentally friendly **herbicides** and facilitating the adoption of **conservation tillage**, GM crops have already contributed to increasing agricultural **sustainability**' (Carpenter, 2011).

A key variable for the environmental performance of GM crops is the amount of pesticides needed compared to the conventional counterparts. Carpenter (2011) quotes one particular survey among farmers, which has shown decreases of up to 75% in the amount of insecticide and/or number of insecticide applications used on Bt crops compared to conventional crops in Argentina, Australia, China, India and the US. In HT crops, the amount of herbicides sprayed often does not change significantly but the advantage for the environment arises from fewer varieties of herbicides that have to be applied.

However, a closer look at the selection of literature in this study unveils that conclusions were mostly drawn from studies on developed countries and do not take into account the long-term effects already discussed above, which could, for example, lead to an overall increase of **pesticide** use with growing resistance of pests and herbs to the GM trait.

from *The Impact of Biotechnology on Developing Countries*
by Timo Kaphengst and Lucy Smith

### Word cloud

biodiversity
biotechnology
conservation tillage
cultivation
herbicide
insecticide
pesticide
sustainability
yields

### Glossary

**socio-economic impacts** the effect on an individual's or group's position within a social structure

**GM crops** genetically modified crops

**conventional crops** those not modified

**facilitating the adoption** enabling the use of

**Carpenter (2011)** study author (date published)

**a key variable** an important factor that may change

**Bt crops** crops modified with *Bacillus thuringiensis* (Bt) which is poisonous to insects

**HT crops** herbicide tolerant crops

## Understanding

This extract from a scientific study on the use of GM crops in agriculture is formal and written in the third person.
**Answer the following questions.**

1. How does the opening paragraph offer a balanced view?
2. What is the subject of the third paragraph?
3. Which words suggest that previous studies may be incorrect?
4. Who do you think is the intended audience for this report?

## Developing your language – building a technical vocabulary

**Read this description then answer the questions.**

First you fill a few plastic things with that mucky stuff and then put some of that wet thingy on them. Put each plastic thing in one of those warm buildings and leave them until these little bits appear. When the little bits have four flat bits take them out of the plastic things and shove them in the bigger plastic thing. Put the wet thingy on them regularly until they're kind of bigger. Then you can shove them in the brown stuff outside.

1. Rewrite the description, substituting the highlighted vocabulary with these technical words.

plant compost seedlings water soil pots
15cm high greenhouses leaves container

2. Why are the instructions easier to follow now?

**Key concept**

**Technical vocabulary is effective because:**

- it demonstrates the writer's knowledge of the subject
- it informs and instructs the reader
- it is accurate and exact in its meaning.

## Word builder

**Look at the Word cloud then answer the questions.**

1. What subject are all the words related to?
2. What does the prefix ***bio-*** suggest about the meaning of the word it is attached to?
3. What do the resulting words mean after adding the prefix '*bio–*' ? Use a dictionary to help you.

sphere psy nics chemical logical pic
degradable graphy

4. If the prefix ***bio-*** suggests a positive connotation, the suffix ***-cide*** has a very different meaning.
What do the words *insecticide, herbicide, pesticide, genocide, patricide, suicide* have in common? Use a dictionary.

## Fitting sentences to purpose

To write more effectively, it is best to vary the way you construct sentences, depending on the purpose and audience.

You can control pace, tone, atmosphere and how much you want the reader to know through your sentence construction.

To **increase the pace/tension** use **short simple sentences.**

To **slow the pace/add lots of additional information** use **compound and complex sentences.**

Look again at the first sentence from the extract about GM crops.

> Similar to the debate on the socio-economic impacts of GM crops adoption, there are different opinions about the potential risks of the cultivation of GM crops for the environment and, in particular, biodiversity.

This is a complex sentence that gives the reader lots of information.

It has **four strands**:

- It links to a debate on a connected theme.
- It introduces the topic under consideration.
- It acknowledges the idea that there are different perspectives.
- It focuses on a particular area to be covered.

Now read this paragraph from the extract about GM crops.

> An often quoted and more recent study based on a literature review on the environmental impacts of GM crops with particular emphasis on biodiversity came to the conclusion that 'by increasing yields, decreasing insecticide use, increasing the use of more environmentally friendly herbicides and facilitating the adoption of conservation tillage, GM crops have already contributed to increasing agricultural sustainability' (Carpenter, 2011).

1. How many sentences are there in this paragraph?
2. What kinds of sentences are used?
3. Why do you think the authors use a quotation?
4. What are the subject and purpose of the paragraph?

**Key concept**

### Writing for a purpose

In the article on the impact of biotechnology on page 40:

The tone and atmosphere have been established as formal and serious.

The pace is even and measured to suggest much thought has gone into the writing.

The use of technical terms assumes that the reader is aware of their meaning.

## Writing your report

Now it is your turn. You are going to write a short report entitled: 'Should we grow GM crops?'

**Preparation**

- Use the internet to research GM crops.
- Make notes on the arguments for and against the use of GM crops.

**Process**

- Acknowledge both sides of the argument.
- Favour only one.
- Use only compound and complex sentences.

**Write:**

- an introductory complex sentence using the four strands on page 42
- a paragraph considering the opposing argument but doubting its credibility
- a paragraph stating why your viewpoint is more credible
- a conclusion summing up your argument.

**Remember**

Remember that there are three main types of sentences you use regularly: simple, compound, and complex. Use only the last two in your report.

## Speaking and listening

### Presenting your report to an audience

It is often the case that a report is presented orally to an audience.

This requires preparation and possibly some minor rewriting to suit the different delivery style as what you write for a reader may not work for a listener.

**a** Read out loud your written report.

**b** Was it easy to read or do some of the sentences need adjusting to make them easier to deliver orally?

**c** Adjust your written report accordingly.

**d** Read it out loud again and repeat the process until you are satisfied.

## Help wanted!

### Word cloud

apocalypse
calamity
cataclysm
catastrophe
debacle
fiasco

### Understanding

Public speaking is considered one of the most stressful and difficult activities, but prepared thoroughly and performed properly, it can be very rewarding.

1. What is the topic of Andrei's speech?
2. Why is Bimla a good person to ask for advice on delivering a speech?
3. What kind of image is 'floundering like a beached whale' and how is it used effectively by Andrei?
4. In your opinion, how useful is the advice given by Bimla concerning successful speeches?
5. If you were to write and deliver a speech, what are the three most important pieces of advice you would take from listening to this text?

### Glossary

**A.I.** artificial intelligence

**scientific conundrum** a riddle worrying scientists

**moral aspects** whether it is right or wrong

**humanoid** of human appearance

**diametrically opposed** direct opposite

**verbal pyrotechnics** (metaphor) spoken fireworks display

**mimics eye contact** appears as if the speaker is looking directly at the audience

## Speaking and listening – hot seating

You are a scientist who believes that artificial intelligence is the answer to all the world's problems.

Your audience is composed of those who believe robots will destroy the world.

The scientist sits in the 'hot seat' and is interviewed by the audience.

## Developing your language – using a thesaurus

Each word in the English language has its own individual definition, but often there are groups of words with a similar meaning. A thesaurus is where you can find these words arranged in alphabetical order.

The following words are all synonyms for the noun ***enunciation***, meaning the act of communicating words clearly.

*articulation* *pronunciation* *diction* *intonation*

Use a thesaurus to find words with similar meanings to:

**a** afraid **b** nervous **c** exhausted

## Word builder

Look at the words in the Word cloud. They are all synonyms for a disaster of some kind. Find the words in the word search below and complete the statements.

| | | | | | | | | | | | |
|---|---|---|---|---|---|---|---|---|---|---|---|
| H | A | P | O | C | A | L | Y | P | S | E | K |
| D | J | C | S | W | H | C | A | T | A | B | C |
| A | E | B | R | Q | H | L | O | I | L | A | A |
| T | Y | B | F | I | A | S | C | O | T | T | Y |
| X | C | V | A | J | U | D | E | A | X | M | T |
| E | Q | Z | C | C | L | W | C | L | Y | S | I |
| R | A | V | N | E | L | L | C | A | H | K | M |
| S | Y | Y | T | S | I | E | T | O | I | R | A |
| W | U | B | R | S | F | D | E | B | A | C | L |
| Q | E | R | M | Y | H | L | V | C | E | D | A |
| E | E | H | P | O | R | T | S | A | T | A | C |
| G | Y | I | T | M | A | L | A | C | H | A | C |

**a** An a________e is an event causing disastrous destruction.

**b** A disaster caused by natural forces is a c________m.

**c** A complete disaster or failure is a f________o.

**d** An event causing a sudden disaster is called a c________y.

**e** The rise of A.I. could become a c________e if left uncontrolled.

**f** A d________e would follow if robots took control.

## Writing and performing a speech

You are going to prepare, write and perform a short speech in response to the question

> Is our increased use of artificial intelligence beneficial or dangerous?

**Preparation**

The first step is to work out the basics.

- Who is my audience?
- Is my purpose to entertain, educate or persuade?
- How long should I talk for?

Now follow these guidelines:

1. Do your research and make notes.
2. Decide which side of the argument you support.
3. Write a short plan linking the ideas you are going to include so they flow smoothly.

Use the writing frame on page 47 to help you put together your speech.

### Looking closely

A speech consists of three parts:

An introduction

The main idea

A conclusion

## Speaking and listening – practice makes perfect

Practising your speech as you are writing it will help you to work on how effective it will be.

1. When you have written a section, practise presenting this to an audience and listen to the feedback you receive.
2. For the main idea, practise after you have written each paragraph.
3. Work out which phrases to emphasise and when to pause. Pausing after using a rhetorical question can be effective, as it allows the audience thinking time.
4. Practising each section will help you to learn the whole speech more easily. Test yourself without your script to find out the parts you need to concentrate on.
5. When you are happy with the content, practise using cue cards to aid you when delivering your speech. Page 47 tells you more about them.

## Speech writing frame

**Introduction:**

What will best gain your audience's attention?

- A rhetorical question
- A fact or statistic
- Your opinion on the question
- Foreshadowing the conclusion

**The main idea:**

- Introduce the counter argument then dismiss it in favour of your own.
- Express your main argument, using examples, quotations and statistics to support your viewpoint.

**Conclusion:**

Listeners remember the end most clearly so it needs to be a powerful conclusion.

- Use a quotation that supports your view.
- Use a rhetorical or leading question to make your audience think.
- Make your viewpoint clear.

**Consider:**

- Have you used the correct tone?
- Are your sentences too long?
- Is your vocabulary accurate?
- Do your quotations and statistics support your points?
- Have you persuaded the audience your view is correct?

**Remember:**

You are writing with the intention of speaking. Practise out loud to make sure your speech works as an oral piece.

**Transitional links:**

Your argument should flow from one point to the next. Use linking phrases to do this such as: *'Having dismissed that theory, it is now possible to explore the real threat A.I. poses.'*

## Preparing cue cards

Most professional speakers learn their speeches but use cue cards to remind them what to say.

A cue card is a small (A6 size) card containing a few notes, quotations and statistics to remind you what to say at certain points in the speech. Cue cards are sometimes called prompt cards.

Here is an example of one for an introduction, showing its features.

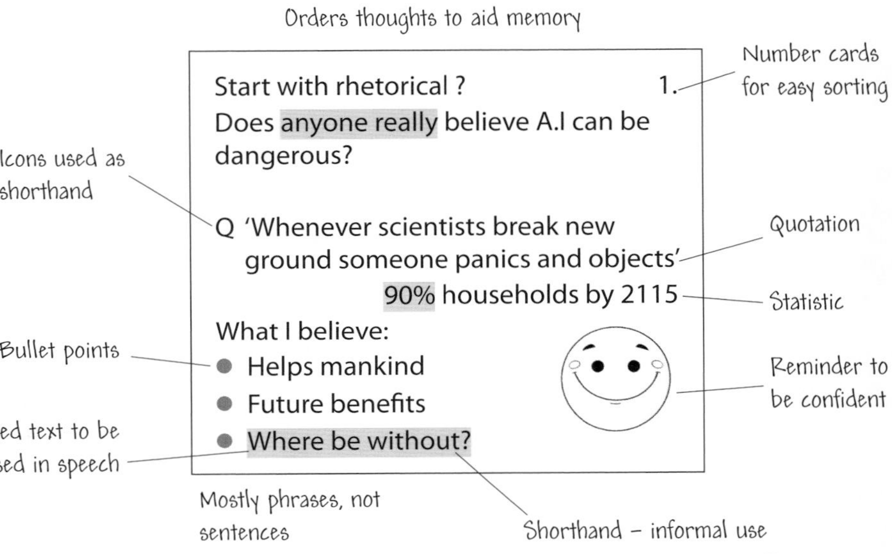

## Progress check

1. In 'The Robots of Dawn', why do the teenagers attack the robot; and who saves it? [2 marks]
2. 'Why do so many people distrust robots?' What type of question is this an example of and how do you know? [2 marks]
3. 'GM crops have already contributed to increasing agricultural sustainability.' What are 'GM crops' and how does this sentence support their use? [2 marks]
4. What do 'cataclysm' and 'catastrophe' have in common? Can you add a third word to the list? [2 marks]
5. What is a thesaurus, and when might using one NOT work? [2 marks]
6. Give four rules that apply to taking part in a constructive argument. [4 marks]
7. Name two differences between an open and a closed question. Give an example of each. [4 marks]
8. What is a rhetorical sentence? Give three ways one might begin. [4 marks]
9. What four tips for public speaking does Bimla suggest in the listening extract? [4 marks]
10. Give four features of a successful cue card. [4 marks]

## Reflecting on your learning

Consider your progress through this unit as being like a crop growing in a field. How far have you grown?

| | | | | |
|---|---|---|---|---|
| I've made a start<br>Still raining<br>Lots of support needed | I've grown a bit<br>Occasional showers<br>A bit less support needed | Growing quite fast now<br>A little cloudy still<br>Occasional support needed | I've grown a lot<br>Mostly sunny<br>Mostly independent | Wonderful flowers<br>Sun, sun, sun<br>I flourished |

### My speech – how did it go?

How successful was your speech, using a sliding scale where 10 is excellent and 1 offers a lot of scope for improvement?

The introduction: I'd give it ___ out of 10 because ____________________

______________________________________________

The main idea: I'd give it ___ out of 10 because ____________________

______________________________________________

The conclusion: I'd give it ___ out of 10 because ____________________

______________________________________________

The audience was: enthusiastic / interested / not interested / bored. (*Choose one*)

The audience: were persuaded by my point of view / disagreed with my point of view. (*Choose one*)

### My action plan: planting the seeds of success

- How can I make my next speech better?
- Did I do enough research, preparation and practice?
- What speaking and listening skills do I need to work on (e.g. tone, fluency, volume, speaking clearly)?
- How am I going to plant the seeds of success?

# 4 Unnatural nature

**In this unit you will:**

**Explore**
- the impenetrable Congolese jungle
- the parched Gobi desert

**Create**
- your own summary
- some personifications

**Engage**
- with the real-life account of a wildlife cameraman
- with some fearsome animals

**Collaborate**
- in conducting a debate
- in a guessing game

**Reflect**
- on the dangers of wild animals
- on the hardships humans face in hostile environments

The most dangerous places on earth?

Nature red in tooth and claw.

Jungles, deserts, and Arctic wastes – they ought to have notices saying 'Keep Out'.

We know everything about this planet – this century should be about exploring the universe!

## Thinking time

1. Look at the pictures on the opposite page. Do you agree with the caption that they are 'the most dangerous places on Earth', or can you think of other equally or more dangerous places where few humans ever go?
2. What do you think about the title 'Unnatural nature'?
3. What do you think the first quotation, 'Nature red in tooth and claw', is about?
4. Do you think there should be no-go areas on our planet for humans or should we be free to go wherever we like?
5. Do you agree with the final quotation: is it just as important to explore the universe as to explore nature?

## Speaking and listening – holding a debate

1. You are going to hold a debate with the motion 'Nature is a playground for us to enjoy'.
2. Two people are needed to start with: one who agrees strongly with the motion (the proposer) and one who disagrees strongly (the opposer).
3. The proposer and the opposer find others who share their view. Now there are two teams – one led by the proposer, the other led by the opposer.
4. The proposer asks the first speaker on his or her team to propose the motion. A second person then backs up this speaker with a supporting idea.
5. The team opposing the motion responds, using the same method.
6. Now there is an opportunity for debate. All responses must be channelled through the team leaders.
7. At the end, the proposer and the opposer sum up the points their teams have made and everyone votes to decide which side has won.

*Debating chamber in Canberra, Australia*

## A terrible place in the jungle

More than a century ago, a brave woman called Mary Kingsley went to West Africa to collect specimens of fish. Read her description of a place called Talagouga.

Talagouga is grand, but its scenery is undoubtedly grim, and its name, **signifying** the **gateway** of misery, seems applicable. It must be a melancholy place to live in, the very air lies heavy and silent. I never saw the trees stirred by a breeze the whole time I was there, and even the broad plantain leaves seemed to stand **sleeping** day out and day in, motionless. (...)

That forest round Talagouga was one of the most difficult bits of country to get about in I ever came across, for it was dense and there were no bush paths. No Fan village wants to walk to another Fan village (...), and all their trade goes up and down the river in canoes. No doubt some miles inland there are bush paths, but I never **struck** one. Neither did I come across any villages in the forest, they seem all to be on the river bank round here. (...)

Now and again on exposed parts of the hillside, one comes across great falls of timber which have been **thrown** down by tornadoes either flat on to the ground – in which case under and among them are snakes and scorpions, and getting over them is slippery work; or thrown sideways and hanging against their fellows, all covered with gorgeous **drapery** of climbing, flowering plants – in which case they present to the human **atom** a **wall** made up of strong tendrils and climbing grasses, through which the said atom has to cut its way with a matchette and push into the crack so made getting, the while covered with red driver-ants, and such like, and having sensational meetings with blue-green snakes, dirty green snakes with triangular horned heads, black cobras, and boa constrictors. I never came back to the station without having been frightened half out of my wits.

From *Travels in West Africa* by Mary Kingsley

### Word cloud

| | |
|---|---|
| atom | sleeping |
| drapery | struck |
| gateway | thrown |
| signify | wall |

### Glossary

**Fan village** a village of the West African Fans tribe

**matchette** a large, heavy knife used as a weapon

**plantain** a plant of the banana family whose fruit is starchy and less sweet and eaten cooked

**tendril** a twisting, slender part of a plant that climbs another plant or object

## Understanding

1. Why do the villagers not want to walk from one village to the next?
2. How do the villagers travel from one place to another?

3. Explain the difficulties caused to humans by the fallen trees.
4. Write two or three sentences to describe Kingsley's feelings about the forest area of Talagouga and her reasons for those feelings.

## Developing your language – images and metaphors

You will probably know some of the words in the Word cloud. They are images being used in the passage as metaphors – words or phrases that flash a picture into your imagination. This helps to create a mental picture of Talagouga.

For example, Kingsley says that the leaves 'stand sleeping' all day. Leaves don't sleep, so she must mean that they looked like the shape of some sort of animal sleeping and not moving.

Now you have a go. Think of an animal or object. Try and describe it using a metaphor that is also a strong image. For instance, you could describe monkeys as 'the gymnasts of the jungle'.

Metaphors can catch you out when you are reading because they can mean something that seems different from what is being described. They are there to make the picture clearer, but you have to use your thinking skills to work out the relationship of the metaphor to the detail being described.

**Remember**

Imagery is the process of using words to create a picture in the mind of the reader.

*Gymnasts of the jungle*

## Word builder

1. Walls are usually made of stone or brick, so why does Kingsley say that the walls were made of tendrils and grasses?
2. When Kingsley says the trees were thrown down by tornadoes, it makes the storms sound human. Why is this imagery effective?
3. You strike objects in anger, but how do you strike a path (i.e. what does the phrase mean)?
4. A gateway is usually an entrance made of metal or stone. Talagouga is a forest where there are no paths, so why does Kingsley tells us that its name includes *gateway*?
5. *Drapery* is an old word used to describe fine materials for furnishings, so why are flowers described as drapery?
6. Atoms are many, many times smaller than humans, so why use *atom* to describe someone climbing up the wall of tendrils and grasses?

## Verb tenses

A tense tells you whether something is happening:

now – in the present    then – in the past    or still to come – in the future.

### Simple present tense and simple past tense

Here is the simple present tense.

Every day in Talagouga I get up promptly at half past six. I have my breakfast of bread and fruit and make my way into the forest. I wear stout boots because there are no paths and I have to climb over fallen logs. I carry my machete and protect myself against insects and those frightening snakes.

Here is the simple past tense.

I found the forest a forbidding place and local people rarely walked through it. Instead they went everywhere by canoe. They visited different villages and carried out trade with their neighbours. However, I needed to venture into the jungle, which is where I discovered the specimens of natural life I wished to collect.

**Answer the following questions.**

1. Pick out the one-word verbs in the two extracts above.
2. Look at the first extract and find five verbs, other than *find* and *go*, that do not simply add *–ed* to the simple present to make them simple past. How do they change?
3. Work in pairs. One of you reads the first extract aloud. Then the other person reads it again, but this time in the past tense. Swap roles for the second extract, with the second person repeating it in the present tense.

**Looking closely**

You only need one word for the simple present tense and one for the simple past. For example, 'I wear' is the simple present, and 'I wore' is the simple past.

### Continuous tense

Here is another tense – the continuous tense.

Dear Alice, I am sitting watching the insects which are flying backwards and forwards around the fire.

Dear Alice, Yesterday we were climbing over some dead trees and the rain was falling so hard that we were streaming like waterfalls!

Dear Alice, Tomorrow I am planning to attend a climbing course where I will be learning how to free climb.

**Remember**

Many verbs form their past tenses by adding *–ed* to the present, but some are irregular. For example, *find* becomes *found* and *go* becomes *went*.

**Answer the following questions.**

1. What do you notice about how the continuous tense works?
2. 'Tomorrow, I will learn how to free climb.' How is this different from the third letter's opening?

## Understanding

**Answer the following questions.**

1. Which tense would you probably use to write about these topics?
   - **a** Information about the place where you live
   - **b** A story about someone who went into the jungle
   - **c** A description of what you see as you look down the street
   - **d** Information about a town you are going to relocate to
2. Imagine you are the teacher and a student wrote this description.

   As I sat lazily in front of my house, I see a giraffe slowly making its way across the dusty road. Some children playing in the road will stop and have stood to watch. The giraffe stops too and stretched its neck to investigate a tree that borders the road. It did not find what it wants, appears to make a little bow and will disappear from sight.

   Decide how you would correct this description then write your version.
3. What advice would you give to the student for writing a description in the future?

## Speaking and listening – a guessing game

### Twenty questions

Only use the simple present tense or the present continuous tense during this game.

The quiz leader thinks of an object connected to nature. Others have to guess what it is by asking questions such as:

"Is it an animal?" "Can you eat it?" "Does it live in the sea?"

If you use the past or future tense, the quiz leader says "No". When those guessing have been told "No" twenty times, the quiz leader wins.

When guessing, listen carefully to the information given in the answers and use it wisely. Take it in turns to be quiz leader.

### Looking closely

When you are writing, it is important to decide which tense you are going to use. You use continuous tenses when you write about things that don't just happen once, but are happening all the time.

## Water! Water! Find me water!

Some desperately hungry and thirsty travellers suddenly see what might be an oasis in the Mongolian desert.

### The Gobi Desert: Saved by an oasis

It took us a good two hours to make the intervening distance. Many times we lost sight of the thing we sought as we plunged along in the sandy depressions. We climbed more often than we would otherwise have done because we could not bear the idea that somehow the smudge on the landscape might disappear while we were cut off from view of it. It began to take shape and definition and hope began to well up in us. And hope became certainty. There were *trees* – real, live, growing, healthy trees, in a **clump**, outlined against the sand like a blob of ink on a fresh-laundered tablecloth.

"Where there are trees there is water," said the American.

"An oasis," someone shouted, and the word fluttered from mouth to mouth.

Kristina whispered, "It is a miracle. God has saved us."

If we could have run we would have done so. We toiled that last half-mile as fast as we could flog our legs along. I went sprawling a few times. My tongue was dry and swollen in my mouth. The trees loomed larger and I saw that they were palms. In their shade was a sunken **hollow**, roughly **oval-shaped**, and I knew this must be water. A few hundred yards from the oasis we crossed an east-west caravan track. On the **fringe** of the trees we passed an incongruous pile of what looked like rusting biscuit tins like some fantastic mid-desert junk yard. In the last twenty yards we quickened our pace and I think we managed a lope that was very nearly a run.

The trees, a dozen or more of them, were arranged in a **crescent** on the south side of the pool, and threw their shadow over it for most part of the day. The wonderful cool water lay still and inviting in an **elliptical** depression **hemmed** round with big, **rough-worked** stones. At this time, probably the hottest season, the limits of the water had receded inwards from the stone ring, and we had to climb over to reach it. The whole, green, life-giving spot could have been contained inside half-an-acre.

From *The Long Walk* by Slavomir Rawicz

**Word cloud**

clump
crescent
elliptical
fringe
hemmed
hollow
oval-shaped
rough-worked

## Glossary

**caravan track** the marks left by a group of people travelling across a desert

**depressions** sunken places or hollows in the ground

**incongruous** not in keeping with the surroundings

**lope** walk or run with a long stride

## Understanding

1. What made the travellers think they might find water?
2. What difference had it made that it was the hot season?
3. Give two reasons why the travellers were in a poor state.
4. List the various emotions of the travellers as they are described.

## Developing your language – describing locations

Writers are experts in using words that give an exact picture of a place.

The first paragraph of the extract refers to the intervening distance. The trees first appear as a 'smudge' – a metaphor suggesting a patch with no definite shape. As the travellers get nearer, the smudge becomes a clump, a group of recognisable trees.

The simile 'like a blob of ink on a freshly laundered tablecloth' tells us that the trees stood out clearly from their surroundings.

**Answer the following questions.**

1. What locations would you use for the following stories?
   - **a** You take a short cut and get home late because you get lost.
   - **b** A robber escapes with a haul of jewels.
   - **c** A crowd assembles to watch a race go by.
2. Now create a simile to enhance your location – to make readers feel they can see it.

## Word builder

Now look closely at the last two paragraphs of the extract from *The Long Walk*.

1. What do *fringe* and *crescent* tell you about the trees?
2. What do *elliptical*, *hollow* and *oval-shaped* tell you about the place where the water lay?
3. What do *hemmed* and *rough-worked* tell you about the appearance of the water hole?
4. Use as many of the words in the Word cloud as you can to describe a completely different setting.

**Remember**

Similes compare two things that are not alike by using connectives such as *like* and *as*. They are more straightforward than metaphors, which try to equate the two things being compared.

### Speaking and listening

You turn a corner at the top of a hill and see an unusual sight ahead of you. You do not know what it is at first but as you get nearer, all becomes clear. Be prepared to tell your story!

**Remember**

Remember to use images in your own writing to make readers feel they are there. Images used effectively in similes or metaphors will add to the impression you create.

# The conditional tense

## Working with conditional tenses

Here are two examples of use of the conditional tense:

If it gets any hotter, the oasis will run dry.

If it were to rain tomorrow, the oasis would fill up.

**Practise the conditional tense by answering these questions.**

**1.** Copy and complete these sentences:

- **a** If we heat ice, ______________________________ ______________________________.
- **b** If I stroke my cat too hard, ______________ ______________________________.
- **c** If I walk for too long in the sun, __________ ______________________________.

**2.** Now write some of your own conditionals based on these settings:

- **a** a ship in the sea
- **b** an avalanche on a mountain
- **c** waking up a sleeping lion in the jungle.

**3.** Write a definition of the conditional tense in one sentence.

**4.** Copy and complete these sentences:

- **a** If we were to be hit by an iceberg, ______________.
- **b** If my cat were to eat a mouse, ______________.
- **c** If I were never to go in the sun, ______________.

**5.** Now write some of your own similar conditional sentences based on:

- **a** riding a horse across a water-jump
- **b** driving a car much too fast
- **c** visiting a new and strange place.

**6.** In a sentence, how are the following conditionals different from your previous ones?

If you had told me the oasis was dry, I would have brought water.

## The conditional tense – more examples

**For more practice in using the conditional tense, answer these questions.**

1. Complete these sentences:
   - a If the world had no ice. . .
   - b If you had told me about that cat. . .
   - c If I had known about the heat. . .
2. Now write two or three sentences, using the conditional tense, starting:
   - a If I were accidentally locked in the school library. . .
   - b If I had not forgotten my homework. . .
   - c If that rope bridge across the river gives way. . .

Now look at your sentences from question 2 and see how they have developed your understanding of the conditional tense. You may have noticed that conditionals tend to work in these three situations:

using the present tense with the consequence = very likely result using the future

using the past tense with the consequence = uncertain result using *would* or *should*

using a tense called the perfect tense = cannot be proven

### Looking closely

Conditionals are sometimes called '*if* clauses'. Some conditionals describe real-life situations and others describe imaginary situations. Use them to make your stories more interesting.

### Speaking and listening

In groups, take turns to role-play one or two examples of the first conditional, the second conditional, and the third conditional. Choose nature settings.

The first conditional starts by stating something quite likely, for example: 'If I go closer to that forest fire, I will be burned.'

The second conditional adds a less likely scenario, for example: 'If that forest fire had started three weeks ago in the rainy season, it would have been put out quickly.'

The third conditional adds the impossible to prove, for example: 'If I had known there was going to be a fire, I would have worn a fire-proof suit today.'

It's not an easy game to play, so have some fun exploring and finding your way – a little like you would in a jungle!

## Wild animals caught on camera

| | |
|---|---|
| ambushed | malevolent |
| grips | sever |
| layers | squirm |

Listen to this recording. In it, Olaf tells some students how he came to take some exciting pictures of wild animals and found himself in dangerous situations. You will need to listen to the recording carefully and make short notes to answer question 5 below. You will use these notes later in the writing workshop.

### Glossary

**a real buzz** great excitement

**click, click and I'm off** taking photos before running away quickly from potential danger

**jungle creeper** plants that grow and spread out along the ground and up trees

**one huge sweep** large, scooping action

## Understanding

**Answer the following questions.**

1. Why doesn't Olaf use a close-up lens?
2. What saved Olaf from being noticed by the leopard?
3. Olaf says, "OK, so I'm an idiot". Write four words that describe Olaf's character (not including 'idiot').
4. What do you think about Olaf's craze for animal photography at close range?
5. Make notes of the facts given about hippopotamuses, leopards and crocodiles. There's no need to put your notes in any particular order – there will be time to do that later.

### Speaking and listening

You are going to pretend to be Olaf. At the end of your speech you will take some questions from students in the audience. Try to predict the questions they may ask.

## Developing your language – personification

Olaf wants his language to create as strong an impression as his photographs. The words in the Word cloud suggest danger and tell us that the natural world is full of peril. These words are all connected to a type of image called personification – an abstract idea that is made into a person.

Read this extract from the recording.

> 'Here was I looking Death in the face again – and Death had layers of teeth like pointed nails and dreadful claws that would sever you apart.'

Olaf creates an impression of danger by making you imagine dreadful claws and giving an image of pointed nails for teeth. The word *sever* suggests a violent pulling of flesh from bone.

**Answer the following questions.**

1. If Death were a person, how would you describe him or her?
2. If Death were an animal, which one would it be?
3. Can you think of a way to personify life?
4. Can you think of a way to personify winter?

Key concept

### Personification

Personification can work at two levels: it can give an animal the characteristics of a human, and it can give an abstract thing the characteristics of a human or an animal.

**Examples:**

The bees played hide and seek in the flowers.

The branches waved in the wind.

## Word builder

How do the words in the Word cloud contribute to three other personifications in Olaf's talk?

1. "Danger and I are old enemies – he's ambushed me and threatened me with his daggers more than once, I can tell you." How does *ambushed* help to create the image of danger as a person?
2. "I've never felt the presence of fear. Fear grips you by the throat and makes you squirm and tremble until you can't do anything." How do *grips*, *squirm* and *tremble* help to create the image of fear as a person?
3. "I think of nature as a malevolent ogre ready to pounce on her prey and strike him dead." How does *malevolent* help to create the image of nature as an ogre?

## Writing a summary

**Remember**

A summary is a record of the main points of something you have read, seen or heard.

**Answer the following questions.**

1. Read this summary of everything someone did one Monday, described in only 100 words.

   Monday was the first day of the holidays so I lay in. I got up at midday and had a quick meal before going out to meet my friends. We decided to go to the cinema and then had a coffee while we waited for the rain to stop. When the sun came out we went for a walk by the river and went in the butterfly house. Then it was time to go home. I had my evening meal and sat down and read a book. Before I knew it, it was time to go to bed again.

   What do you notice about this summary that is different from other types of writing, such as more detailed description or a story?

2. Here are some notes about why Olaf was in danger.

   Gets very near to wild animals

   Hippo charged him fast

   Hippo may crush him

   Leopard could rip him with sharp claws

   Leopard could sink teeth into him

   Nearly knocked into river by crocodile's tail

   What do you notice about these notes?

3. Do you think this is an acceptable summary of the notes?

   **Summary based on the notes** – 56 words long

   Olaf was in danger because he got too close to wild animals. He was charged by a hippopotamus that could have crushed him to death. If the leopard had noticed him he might have been a victim to its tearing claws and its sharp teeth. He narrowly missed being knocked into the river by a crocodile.

## Summaries – true or false?

Decide whether each of these statements about summaries is 'True' or 'False', referring to the summary you have just read on page 62.

|  | | |
|---|---|---|
| Summaries start with a long introduction that states what they're about. | TRUE | FALSE |
| I can put explanations and examples wherever I like when writing a summary. | TRUE | FALSE |
| Summaries are about facts and information. | TRUE | FALSE |
| Summaries are just lists so it doesn't matter about the order in which I write. | TRUE | FALSE |
| I don't have to use my own words to write a summary, I can just copy from the original. | TRUE | FALSE |

You use summaries every day. If your mum says, "What did you do at school?", a good answer would be a summary. Keep to the point and keep it short. Use your own words to make everything clear.

Now find your notes giving facts about hippopotamuses, leopards and crocodiles. Write your own summary as follows.

### Plan your summary

Decide the best order for your notes.

### Start your summary

Start with a sentence that gets you straight into the summary, for example:

*Olaf, the wildlife cameraman,...*

### Write the main part of your summary

Keep to the facts, but try to avoid making your summary a basic list. Use your own words to link your factual information together.

Write your summary in a single paragraph of not more than 100 words.

### Finish your summary

Check how many words you have written. If there are too many, see whether you can make your summary shorter by striking out words you don't need, or by writing one word that means the same as two.

## Progress check

1. What do you think 'Nature red in tooth and claw' really means? Give two ideas. [2 marks]
2. Why was Talagouga called the 'Gateway of Misery'? Give two reasons. [2 marks]
3. From the extracts about Talagouga, can you remember two reasons why travel other than by water was very difficult? [2 marks]
4. Why did the travellers across the Gobi Desert say that the trees were 'outlined against the sand like a blob of ink on a freshly laundered tablecloth'? [2 marks]
5. What did Olaf the cameraman say Mother Nature was not, and how did he describe her? [2 marks]
6. Explain the type of imagery Olaf was particularly fond of using. Give two examples. [4 marks]
7. In a debate what is meant by a motion, a proposer, and an opposer? How are people prevented from talking all at once? [4 marks]
8. Can you remember how the setting of the oasis in the Gobi Desert was described? Give four details. [4 marks]
9. Choose two conditional tenses and give an example showing how they differ from each other. [4 marks]
10. State four rules for writing a summary. [4 marks]

## Reflecting on your learning

### Writing summaries

| | |
|---|---|
| I understand the main rules for writing summaries. | ☐ Yes, and I get them right<br>☐ Yes, but I forget some of them<br>☐ I find them a bit confusing |
| I can find the information I need to use for the question. | ☐ I can read for detail and know when I've found the right bits<br>☐ I miss some bits out<br>☐ I don't always choose the right bits |
| I'm able to change the wording into my own. | ☐ I enjoy the challenge<br>☐ I sometimes copy the odd phrase<br>☐ I tend to copy a lot |
| I can reduce a passage to the right number of words. | ☐ I'm quite a concise writer<br>☐ I tend to want to add too many words<br>☐ My writing can be too long or too short |
| When I've finished, I have strategies for reducing words. | ☐ I can say things in different ways<br>☐ It takes me some time to think how to change my words<br>☐ I need to broaden my vocabulary |

Focus on the areas you need to improve.

- What types of reading should I be doing to help me to write summaries?
- In the next few weeks, what can I work at most when I am writing summaries?
- In the longer term, how will I know that my plans for improvement have succeeded?

# 5 Fabulous hobbies

**In this unit you will:**

**Explore**
- the purpose of an editorial
- how magazines are aimed at target audiences

**Create**
- a review or report
- a themed magazine for your school

**Engage**
- with a range of sports and hobbies popular across the world
- with the alternative lifestyle of an Ultimate Frisbee player

**Collaborate**
- to plan a school magazine with a specific theme
- to edit an article for the magazine

**Reflect**
- on when to use formal and informal language
- on the use of a range of punctuation for accuracy and effect

Everyone has a hobby of some kind. You just have to find the right one for you.

I love reading our school magazine; it tells us what we want to know.

Sometimes it's just good to chill, find out the gossip, and maybe learn a little too.

## Thinking time

A school magazine project can be a really effective way to learn about journalistic writing and the variety of non-fiction texts that exist. Giving the magazine a theme, such as 'sports and hobbies', makes it more inviting to readers.

1. What kind of magazines do you like to read?
2. Do you agree that everyone has some kind of hobby?
3. Reading is often considered a solitary activity, but how might it be a way to socialise with friends too?
4. For a school magazine to be attractive to you, what kind of material would it need to include?
5. How could you make a magazine that features sports and hobbies as its main theme equally inviting to both males and females in your school?

During this unit you are going to plan and write your own school magazine. It is going to have 'sports and hobbies' as its main theme but can include a wide variety of all kinds of non-fiction texts, such as articles, editorials, extracts from blogs, reports and adverts.

## Speaking and listening

Publishers of magazines invest a lot of money, time, and effort in thoroughly researching the potential market before launching a new magazine. This is called ***market research***.

Before you begin your market research, you need to hold an editorial meeting to discuss how you are going to proceed.

Consider these questions:

1. Who is your target audience? Is it the whole school or certain age groups?
2. What do you want to include in your magazine? (*At this stage consider a variety of ideas.*)
3. How will you make it attractive for both males and females within your target audience?
4. What size, length and format should it be? (*Don't be too ambitious – think practically.*)
5. What is the best name for it? (*Agree on a working title.*)

**Remember**

Remember that this is a planning stage. There will be plenty of time to make changes and final decisions later.

## Editorials

### Setting the tone – where to begin

This is the calendar of editorials for a school magazine called *Carpe Diem*. The lead editorial sets the tone for the issue and the others introduce particular sections.

| *Carpe Diem* 2016 editorial schedule | | | |
|---|---|---|---|
| | **Lead editorial** | **Sports and hobbies challenge** | **General interest editorial** |
| **Spring term** | A new year; a new resolution! Avoid **indecision** | Time to try something new | Are we **insecure** without our mobile phones? |
| **Summer term** | There is a 'me' in *team* | You don't have to be a team player to love sports | Being **independent**; choosing your own path |
| **Autumn term** | The benefits of extra-curricular activities | Love exercise: love life | Do a good deed and earn credits as well |

**Word cloud**

indecision
independent
insecure

**Glossary**

**carpe diem** to use your time wisely by taking your opportunity when it arises; Latin for 'seize the day'

### Understanding

*Carpe Diem* is a 30-page school magazine run by students that publishes monthly. It runs three editorials per issue; one for each section of the magazine.

1. How is the Summer term 'Sports and hobbies challenge' editorial linked to the lead editorial?
2. Which general interest editorials do you think would be of most interest to students in your school?
3. Do you think *Carpe Diem* is a suitable name for the magazine? What message is it trying to convey to its readers?
4. What kind of content do you think the Autumn term editorial 'Love exercise: love life' may contain?

## Developing your language – the prefix 'in-'

If you add the prefix 'in-' to a word, it changes to the opposite meaning.

It is **appropriate** to remain silent when a golfer takes a shot on a golf course.

It is **inappropriate** to shout when a golfer is about to play a shot.

1. Change the meaning of each sentence by adding the prefix ***in-*** to the highlighted word. Some rearrangement of the sentence may be necessary.

   **a** The player's wages were ***adequate*** for someone of his ability.

   **b** The ski slope was only ***accessible*** by cable car.

   **c** It is ***advisable*** to wear a safety helmet when riding a trail bike.

   **d** The ***decisive*** defenders prevented the opposition from scoring.

   **e** Being ***articulate*** is a very important skill for a referee.

   **f** Inter Milan's key defender was ***eligible*** for the game, as his ban had been reduced.

2. Not all words that begin with the letters ***in-*** are words where a prefix has been added. Which of these do not contain prefixes? Use a dictionary.

| | | | |
|---|---|---|---|
| inept | | indecent | |
| | indigo | | inaudible |
| indirect | | inert | |
| | indulgent | | indisposed |
| inevitable | | instinct | |

### Looking closely

An editorial introduces the theme that will run through the present edition of the magazine. It also sets the tone so it will include the editor's opinions about the chosen theme.

## Formal and informal register

To entertain and inform its readers, a magazine will contain a variety of texts and writing styles. Some will be formal but others will be more informal. The balance will depend on the target audience and the purpose of each text.

A general rule to follow is: the more serious a piece of writing, the more formal the tone you use.

### Formal writing

- Is normally written in the third person narrative
- Avoids using second person pronouns
- Uses a more passive voice
- Uses longer, more complex sentences
- Uses sentence structure (syntax) correctly
- Uses vocabulary found in a dictionary and spelt correctly
- Uses punctuation correctly
- Avoids colloquialisms, abbreviations, and contractions
- Creates a more serious tone

### Informal writing

- Can use first, second, or third person narrative
- Uses second person pronouns
- Uses a more active voice
- Contains more simple sentences
- May not follow the rules for syntax
- May use vocab not found in a dictionary and mzpellins
- Uses punctuation for effect!!!
- Creates a less serious tone

### Using first, second and third person narrative

First person is less formal and more personal and engages the reader directly: *I am going to tell you why I became an athlete.*

Second person addresses the reader directly and rarely uses the passive voice: *You need to be physically fit to be an athlete.*

Third person is more impersonal and uses the passive voice more frequently: *Becoming an athlete requires a good level of fitness.*

**Decide which narrative voice has been used and whether the register is formal, semi-formal or informal.**

1. Dedication is required for an athlete to compete at the top level.
2. It's up to you how hard you train.
3. I'm unable to help you if you don't want to help yourself.
4. Not many athletes make it to the Olympics but your chances are good.
5. I ran a personal best for the 100 metres last week.

Key concept

### Similes, metaphors, and idioms

A **simile** is a way of comparing a person or thing to something else, using words such as *like* and *as*.

Example: As brave as a lion.

A **metaphor** describes a person or thing as if they were something else, without using a comparison word.

An **idiom** is a phrase which has a meaning that cannot be worked out from the meanings of the words in it. Example: 'In hot water' means 'in trouble'.

drop the ball
move the goalposts
knock for six
out for the count
stumped
throw in the towel
throw a curve ball

to change the rules
to mislead, deceive
defeated
to give up
to make a mistake
to surprise or shock
deeply asleep

## Similes, metaphors, and idioms

**Answer the following questions.**

1. Match the sporting idioms in the blue panel to their meanings in the red panel. You may find the internet useful.
2. Identify the two positive idioms in **1**.
3. Here are some more idioms used in sports as well as everyday conversation. Unfortunately they have become confused. Can you match them up so they make sense?

| Idiom | Literal meaning | Metaphorical meaning |
|---|---|---|
| Break your duck | Like a plant or tree with roots in one place | To achieve success after a history of failure |
| Don't count your chickens | Only the basic material is left | All is equal |
| Down to the wire | To win by a small part of the body | Stuck and unable to move |
| A level playing field | Six of one and another six of something else | To succeed by the smallest margin |
| To win by a nose | Do not count your feathered livestock | It is up to you |
| Rooted to the spot | The ball is in a space you are playing in | The outcome will not be decided until the very last minute |
| Six of one, half a dozen of the other | To damage a water fowl you own | It is equally both sides' fault |
| The ball is in your court | A flat space on which to play | Don't assume anything |

### Looking closely

Sports journalism uses many idioms. They can be serious but are often humorous.

# A host of hobbies!

## Handy holiday hobby hints

Now that school's nearly over for another year, what will you be doing this summer? Why not try something different for a change? With the whole summer to practise, you have the **opportunity** to learn a new skill and shine at it. If you're looking for **inspiration**, check out these handy hints below.

### Outdoor opportunities

The great outdoors is there to be enjoyed, whether it's exploring new places on organised hiking, biking and camping trips, or **engaging** in a wide range of sports. Football is popular all year round, but there are also summer games such as volleyball, tennis, and track and field events, and water-based activities including swimming, sailing and kayaking. You might enjoy **participating** as part of a team, or prefer something you can do as an individual – the choice is yours!

### Adventures in the arts

Perhaps you've always wanted to try something **creative**? It can be really **satisfying** to create a piece of art which others can enjoy, and gives you the chance to let your **imagination** run wild, using different art forms such as painting, pottery, sculpture and ceramics. Or maybe performance art is more your thing? You could join a local drama group, and try your hand at acting, directing or writing a play. And for the musically minded, try **perfecting** an instrument as your summer goal.

Whatever you choose, be sure to give it your best shot and you might learn a new skill for life. Just remember to be safe, and have fun doing it!

**Word cloud**

creative
engage
imagination
inspiration
opportunity
participate
perfect
satisfy

### Glossary

**shine at it** be the best

**track and field** athletic events that take place on a running track and a nearby field

**let your imagination run wild** don't set any limits

**try your hand at** give something new a try

**give it your best shot** stay focused and try your hardest

## Understanding

1. According to the article, what types of activities might interest a young person?
2. In what narrative voice is the article written?
3. What technique has the author used in the heading and sub-headings?

## Speaking and listening – using vocabulary to set the mood

The 'host of hobbies' article is written to inform the reader about a range of recreational opportunities. It seeks to engage the reader by asking questions and creating a positive tone. One of the ways it does this is through the vocabulary chosen.

All the words in the Word cloud and the phrases in the Glossary help to establish the positive tone.

1. This speech is not so positive. Pick out the negative vocabulary that sets an altogether different tone:

   I have tried countless times to come to terms with fishing as a hobby. I can't take to it. All those mind-numbingly boring hours of staring pointlessly into freezing cold water on the slightest off-chance that a fish will actually swim near the line are tedious beyond my ability to continue anymore. Of course they don't come near. Why would they? Then they'd be as gullible as I am!

2. Write and perform a short speech on the benefits of fishing. Here are five words you can use:
   *relaxing* *peaceful* *calming* *challenging* *rewarding*

## Word builder

Look at the Word cloud. All the words are positive and help to build the overall 'can do' tone in the article.

1. Match the opposites for the pairs to make more sense.

| | |
|---|---|
| inspiration | unpleasant |
| creative | opting out |
| engaging | unimaginative |
| participating | discouragement |
| satisfying | dismissive |

2. You have been tasked to write an article about a sport or hobby you really like. Create your own positive vocabulary list to use in your article.

## Using punctuation accurately

### Colons

Colons are used to introduce an example or explanation within a sentence. For example:

> The leading goal scorer at the 2014 World Cup played for Colombia: James Rodiguez scored five goals.
>
> All Brazilians love football: 'It is in our hearts, our minds and our souls' is a phrase often heard.

In the first sentence, the extra explanation tells you the player's name and how many goals he scored. In the second sentence, the text after the colon gives an example to support the statement.

Colons are also used to introduce a list:

> The following players have all played for Brazil: Neymar, Marcelo, David Luiz and Thiago Silva.

1. Look at these sentences. Which use colons correctly and which don't?
   - **a** The captain of the 1970 World Cup winning team: was called Carlos Alberto Torres.
   - **b** Brazil lost in the semi-final: they finished fourth in the 2014 World Cup.
   - **c** All played their part in the victory: the players, manager, coaches, and backroom staff.
   - **d** A skilful player: Pele could tackle as well as anyone in the team.
   - **e** The oldest person in the stadium was a Brazil fan: He was aged 95.
2. Decide where to put the missing colons in this passage. There are three to insert.

> The Brazilian national team, who play in the famous yellow and green shirts to reflect the colours on the national flag, are the most successful in World Cup history with five wins 1958, 1962, 1970, 1994, and 2002. Whilst the team has included many stars, Pele is the most famous player of all he is widely regarded by those knowledgeable about football as the greatest player of all time. Other great players are heroes in Brazil Carlos Alberto, Jairzinho, Tostão, Gérson, and Garrincha.

**Remember**

A colon indicates that an example, explanation or list is being used by the writer within the sentence.

## Brackets and dashes

A **parenthetical clause** is a phrase that is inserted in a sentence to give extra information. Parenthetical clauses can be separated using brackets (parentheses) or dashes (–). For example:

The leading goal scorer at the 2014 World Cup (James Rodiguez, playing for Colombia) scored five goals.

The leading goal scorer at the 2014 World Cup – James Rodiguez, playing for Colombia – scored five goals.

When used in pairs, dashes are stronger than brackets and can show a change of subject or a break in thought.

I don't mind telling you – and don't think I am being argumentative – that the 1970 World Cup was the best ever.

In this example there is more than just extra information being added, there is also an opinion.

Another purpose of the single dash is to add more information:

That 1970 cup-winning team was the best I've ever seen – oh, and the 1986 team.

**Answer the following questions.**

1. Decide whether brackets or dashes should be used in each of these sentences and where they should go.
   - **a** The World Cup the biggest tournament in sport is held every four years.
   - **b** Germany the first European team to succeed outside Europe won the World Cup in 2014 that is a fact!
   - **c** The first world cup winner way back in 1930 was Uruguay they've won it twice.
   - **d** It is hard to win a World Cup on home soil only six times has it happened which isn't that often.
2. Create some parenthetical clauses to complete this paragraph.

   FIFA (__________) is the governing body responsible for not only football but also futsal and beach soccer. Futsal* – __________ – has become very popular in recent years. Beach soccer isn't only played on beaches but in land-bound cities too – __________. Whatever the variation, the fact remains millions around the world (__________) participate in the sport every day.

**Remember**

Commas, brackets and dashes (used in pairs) can all separate parenthetical clauses from the main sentences, but dashes can also be used to add information at the end of a sentence.

*Futsal = indoor football

## It's the ULTIMATE thrill!

### Word cloud

24/7
Are you dissing...?
dude
Hold your horses
rap sheet
sitch
the price of fame
totally awesome man

### Glossary

**podcast** a digital audio file made available on the Internet for download (usually to subscribers)

**carpe diem** Latin for 'seize the day'

**Ultimate** fast-paced Frisbee game

**alma mater** a Latin phrase that refers to a school/ college previously attended

**we self-regulate** apply the rules ourselves

**'home-grown' policy** colloquial term for producing good Ultimate players from novices

**IOC** International Olympic Committee

## Understanding

Selina is traditional and quite formal and tries to use Standard English in a correct, formal way. Aamir clearly wants to impress his audience with his 'street style' vocabulary and phrasing. Maybe he tries a little too hard to be successful.

1. What is Ultimate Frisbee?
2. Why does Selina largely avoid contractions in her speech patterns?
3. How does Aamir make Selina feel uncomfortable during the interview and does he do it intentionally?
4. The interview seems to have a rather abrupt conclusion. Why might this be so?
5. Aamir becomes more serious and talks in greater detail when he is describing his sport. What does this tell you about him?

## Developing your language – using the informal for effect

Selina and Aamir use very different conventions when speaking in the interview. Selina has been taught to speak correctly and feels a responsibility to be formal in her role as the interviewer. Aamir has no such concerns and seems keen to be as informal as he can.

Look at these extracts from their opening comments:

ST: **I am** delighted to welcome a very special guest for this edition. **He is** a rising Ultimate star, a local hero and an ex-pupil: **he is** none other than Aamir Rashid.

Selina has three opportunities to use contractions and be less formal but she chooses not to.

AR: **No worries. I'm** always glad to help my *alma mater*. **How're you doing?**

Aamir begins with a colloquialism, continues with a contraction, and ends with an equally informal question. His use of the Latin phrase is clumsy and possibly an attempt to impress the audience.

1. Write a different opening sentence for Selina, in which she uses informal language.
2. Translate Aamir's opening comments into formal Standard English.

### Looking closely

Standard English is the formal use of vocabulary, punctuation, and syntax that would be recognised worldwide. Informal language is not Standard English and should only be used for effect.

### Word builder

1. Look at the words in the Word cloud. They are all examples of informal language used by Aamir.
   - **a** Translate Aamir's phrases into more formal language.
   - **b** Give three other examples of informal language used by Aamir in the interview.
2. These words are Aamir's attempt at being 'cool'. Is this the effect his use of non-standard vocabulary creates?
3. Think of five colloquialisms you use or hear regularly.

### Speaking and listening – role play game

Decide who is going to play the strait-laced (traditional and formal) interviewer and who the interviewee is.

Create a five-minute podcast for your own magazine.

**Remember**

A cliché is a phrase so often used that it has lost its meaning. For example, *a game of two halves* is a football cliché.

## Writing a report

You are going to write a report for your school magazine – so how is it different from a review?

**Review**

- A description of a text or product, e.g. a book, film, play, computer console or game, that includes opinions and bias
- Will make a judgement on the subject reviewed

**Report**

- An account of an event witnessed, e.g. a sporting event, concert, activity
- Includes description, opinion and bias

## Speaking and listening – sharing experiences

Before you plan your own personal report it will be good to share some ideas. Discuss:

- the suitability of suggested subjects
- whether your target audience will be engaged
- the different views on the subjects discussed
- what might make a successful piece of writing.

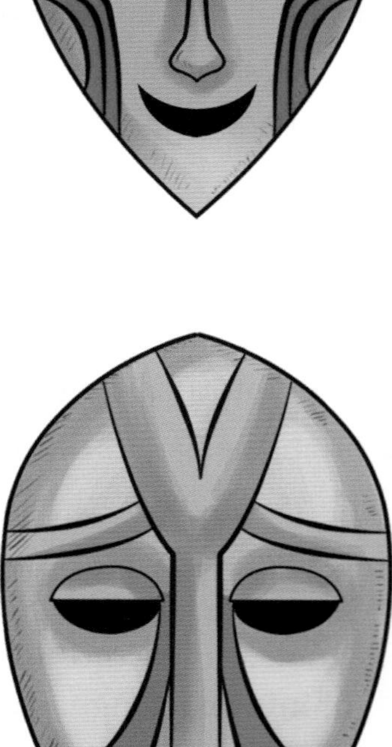

### Planning your piece – five steps to success

1. The first decision to make is the subject of your report.
2. Do some research on your chosen subject. Compile some important facts and, if possible, some quotations you can use.
3. Decide on your bias before starting to write. Are you for or against your subject? Will you be writing to praise or criticise it?
4. Decide on an angle for your piece. What is the significance of you writing about the subject now? (Refer to the 'Significance' box on the next page for guidance.)
5. Make a checklist of the information you think your audience will want to know about your chosen subject, to include in your piece.

Now use the framework opposite to write your piece.

This writing frame will help you to write a successful report for the magazine. It can also be used to write a review.

An interesting opening sentence hooks the reader's attention.

**Opening paragraph:**
Introduce your angle.
Outline the subject.
Prepare the reader for the rest of the piece.

**Significance:**
Is it a new, improved product?
Is it an important match?
Is it worth watching/reading/etc.?

Make clear in the ending what your opinion is.

**Opening sentence:**
Catch the reader's attention.
Introduce the subject.
Introduce narrative voice, e.g. first or third person.

You've got to make the readers think they were there.

**Main body of text:**
Describe the subject.
Offer your opinions.
Maintain your narrative voice.
Entertain the reader.

**The subject:**
Include relevant and accurate facts.
If it is an event, include the most important details.
If it is a review, let the reader know the important details.
State your opinions clearly.
Persuade the reader to agree with your opinions.

If it's good, sell it. If it's bad, make sure no one buys it.

**Be consistent:**
Maintain the same bias consistently.
Keep to one narrative voice.
Maintain a lively style to engage the reader.

**Use quotations from:**
Participants
Interested third parties
Experts
Those who agree with your bias

**Closing paragraph:**
Sum up your opinions.
Make a judgement about your subject.
Make it clear to the reader what you think and why.
If you can, link your comments to your opening paragraph.

Facts must be accurate and opinions must seem like facts to the reader.

## Progress check

1. What is the purpose of an editorial and who would normally write it? [2 marks]

2. Can you remember from what language *Carpe Diem* originates and what it means in English? Choose one answer from each column. [2 marks]

| **Language** | **Meaning** |
|---|---|
| Ancient Greek | There's no hope |
| Latin | Try harder |
| French | Seize the day |
| Russian | Wait for tomorrow |

3. Show why is it better to be a *considerate* interviewer rather than an *inconsiderate* one by explaining what happens when the prefix ***in-*** is added to the front of a word. [2 marks]

4. What are 'slam dunk' and 'out for the count' examples of? Can you think of one other example? [2 marks]

5. What are 'the ball is in your court' and 'to win by a nose' examples of? Can you think of another example? [2 marks]

6. What four qualities do you think make for a successful school magazine? [4 marks]

7. Name two features of formal writing and two different features of informal writing. [4 marks]

8. Can you remember four features of Ultimate Frisbee that appeal to Aamir? [4 marks]

9. Identify two differences between a review and a report. Give an example of a subject for each. [4 marks]

10. Identify four steps to successfully writing a report. [4 marks]

## Reflecting on your learning

### Hurdles to success

Consider your progress through this unit as similar to a hurdles race. Assessing your experience as accurately as you can, how many hurdles have you negotiated?

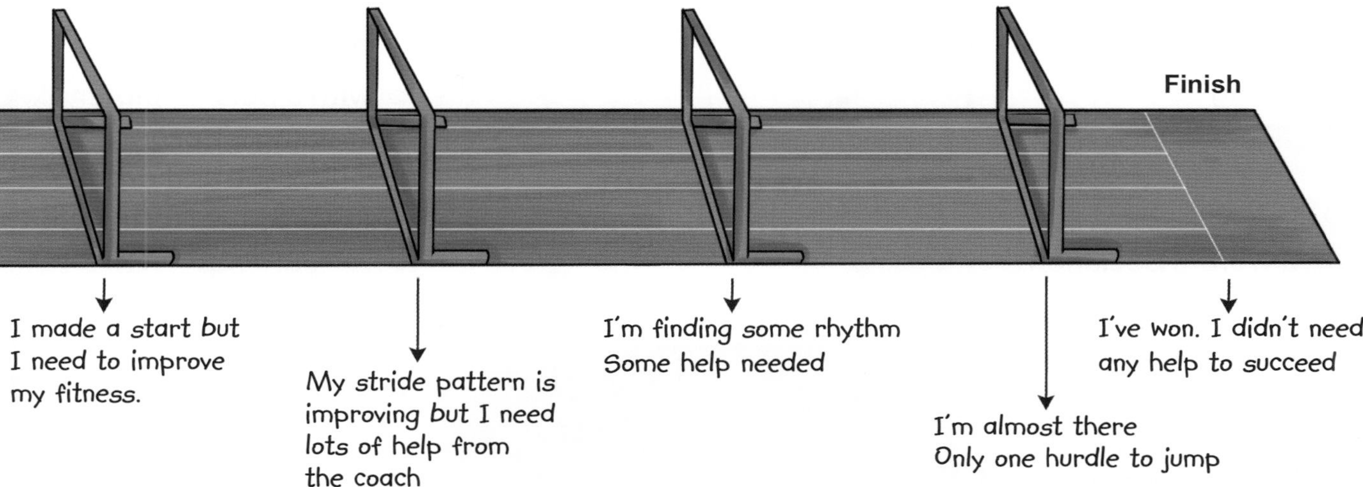


### My action plan: Preparing for a re-run

1. Thinking about how well I negotiated the hurdles race, what do I need to do next to improve my performance?
2. Which of these report writing skills did I struggle with?
   - Maintaining a consistent narrative voice
   - Maintaining a consistent bias
   - Creating an angle
   - Offering relevant opinions
   - Creating an effective introduction
   - Creating an effective conclusion
   - Maintaining a lively style to interest the reader
3. What can I do better to improve my stride pattern and clear more hurdles?
4. How am I going to do this?

# 6 Alarming journeys

**In this unit you will:**

**Explore**
- Mount Everest
- a dangerous river crossing

**Create**
- stories to tell aloud
- mini sagas

**Engage**
- with a mountaineer's thoughts about his climb
- with a polar explorer crossing a frozen landscape and drifting towards the North Pole

**Collaborate**
- in a word-association game
- in writing a short play about a person who loses the ability to spell

**Reflect**
- on what makes you like a poem
- on what makes a journey special or unusual

The way not taken

Journey into space

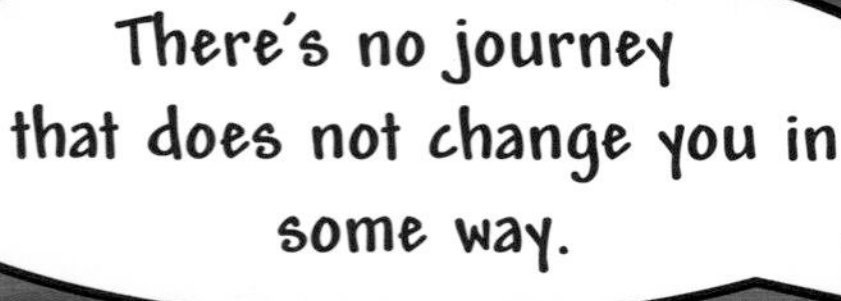


The best journey takes you through your imagination – like a dream!

The best bit of a journey is coming home.

## Thinking time

1. Make a list of all the different sorts of journey you can think of.
2. Do you find journeys fun, boring, exciting, or frightening? Give reasons for your answer.
3. Describe any journey you have imagined taking, or a place you have visited in a dream you have had.
4. What sort of person might say 'The best bit of a journey is coming home'?
5. What do you think is meant by 'there's no journey that does not change you in some way'?

## Speaking and listening

You are going to tell a story. Choose one of the following titles.

- **a** A very short journey I made
- **b** The longest journey I ever made
- **c** The elephant's journey
- **d** The snail's journey

The story will have four sections.

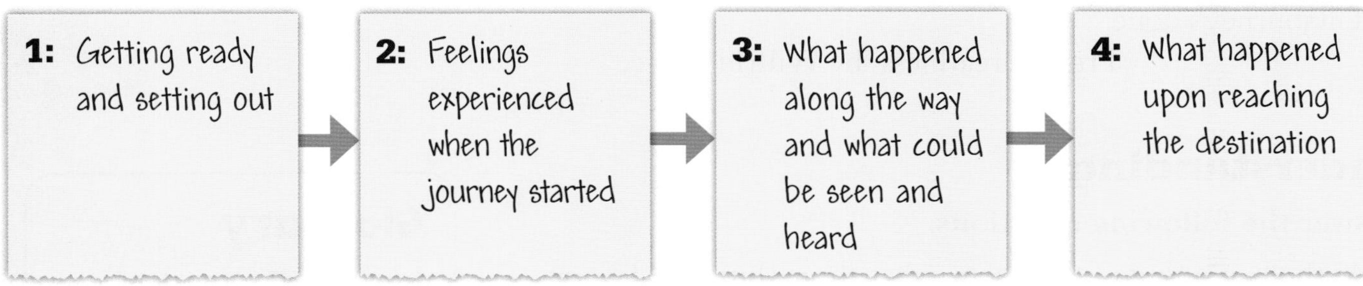


What details can you include to add interest to you story?

## *Conquering Mount Everest*

This poem was written by Wilfrid Noyce, who was a member of the expedition team who first climbed Mount Everest. Noyce wrote the poem while the climb was taking place, on 23 May 1953, when the team was at a height of around 6500 metres.

***Breathless***

Heart aches,
Lungs pant
The dry air
Sorry, **scant**.
Legs lift
And why at all?
Loose drift,
Heavy fall.
**Prod** the snow
Its easiest way;
A flat step
Is holiday.
Look up,
The far stone
Is many miles
Far and alone.
**Grind** the breath
Once more and on;
Don't look up
Till journey's done.
Must look up,
Glasses are dim.
**Wrench** of hand
Is breathless limb.
Pause one step,
Breath swings back;
Swallow once,
Dry throat is **slack**.
Then on
To the far stone;
Don't look up.
Count the steps done.
One step,
One heart-beat,
Stone no nearer
Dragging feet.
Heart aches,
Lungs pant
The dry air
Sorry, scant.

From 'Breathless' by Wilfrid Noyce

grind
prod
scant
slack
wrench

## Understanding

**Answer the following questions.**

1. At the beginning of the poem, what three things make you think that the climb is very difficult for Noyce?
2. What does the poem tell you about the snow?
3. Why does Noyce say 'a flat step is holiday'?
4. Why do you think he does not look up?
5. Why do you think all the lines are so short?
6. Using your imagination, describe how Noyce feels at the end of the poem.

### Glossary

**loose drift** some deep, unstable snow

**a flat step is holiday** not having to go upwards is a great relief

**once more and on** step once more and then carry on

## Developing your language – 'unpacking' words

Some words are like parcels – they need 'unpacking' to find their hidden meanings and associations.

For example, in line 4 of 'Breathless', the writer uses the word *sorry*. With a partner, read this conversation out loud.

Student 1: What does the word 'sorry' suggest to you?'

Student 2: Well, it's usually something someone says. It suggests something was wrong and the person is feeling pretty miserable about it. But this is about oxygen and it suggests that the air is thin. Everything is in a pretty bad way. When I read the line, I sort of know that 'sorry' means all of these things, even if I don't understand the exact meaning.

Here is another example for you to read out loud.

Student 1: The writer says 'breath swings back'. I know what 'swings' means but I've never associated it with breaths.

Student 2: Well, 'swings' is a fairly lively word, like monkeys swinging from a tree. It suggests something healthy – it's associated with dance music. So I suppose it means that he's been seriously out of breath but as soon as he stops, his lungs suddenly fill with air.

Discuss with your partner what you have learnt by reading these two conversations.

**Remember**

Writing words that convey an image will engage a reader. For example, *bush* does not create much of a picture in a reader's mind, but *holly* suggests sharpness, glossiness, a particular shade of green, and red berries that birds like.

### Word builder

Sometimes short words are as difficult to understand as long ones.

Using the approach you took with the two conversations above, work your way through these words from the extract, unpacking them to discover all the associations you can.

**a** prod **b** wrench **c** slack

## Prepositional phrases

Here is a short summary of 'Breathless'.

> Wilfred Noyce was climbing. He had reached a great height when he realised he was suffering. When he looked upwards he wondered whether he had enough energy.

Now read this version with some added prepositional phrases.

> Wilfred Noyce was climbing up Mount Everest. He reached a great height when he realised he was suffering from a shortage of oxygen. When he looked upwards at the far stone he wondered whether he had enough energy for the climb.

**Answer the following questions.**

1. Make a list of the prepositions that join each phrase to its sentence in this summary.
2. Explain carefully what each of the prepositional phrases adds to the original sentence.

There are many prepositions to choose from (see the list opposite), but in your writing be careful to use the right one.

3. Copy the following sentences and complete them using these prepositions: *by*, *with*, *from*, *to*, *for*, or *at*.

   She came to visit me ____________ my lovely new house ____________ the brightly coloured roof. It is situated ____________ the river, not far ____________ the children's playground. I would like to invite you to come ____________ my new house ____________ a long holiday.

4. Now write some sentences that include the following prepositional phrases:
   - **a** in a few minutes
   - **b** with a smile
   - **c** against the old stone wall
   - **d** except every Thursday afternoon
   - **e** with much consideration for his beloved grandchildren
   - **f** with a sudden movement of its sharp claws.

**Remember**

A **phrase** is a few words without a verb that must be joined to a sentence.

A **preposition** is a word that joins a phrase to a sentence.

**Key concept**

### Prepositions

| | |
|---|---|
| about | into |
| above | like |
| across | near |
| after | of |
| against | off |
| along | on |
| among | onto |
| around | out |
| at | outside |
| before | over |
| behind | past |
| below | since |
| beneath | through |
| beside | throughout |
| between | till |
| beyond | to |
| but | toward |
| by | under |
| despite | underneath |
| down | until |
| during | up |
| except | upon |
| for | with |
| from | within |
| in | without |
| inside | |

## Prepositional phrases – adjectives and adverbs

Here is an adjectival prepositional phrase describing a **noun**.

They climbed Mount Everest, the highest mountain in the world.

*Mountain* tells you what Mount Everest is and *in the world* tells you more about the mountain.

Here is an adverbial prepositional phrase describing a **verb**.

Nowadays, many people climb Everest with less difficulty.

*With less difficulty* tells you about how people climb, and *climb* is a verb.

**Key concept**

### Possessive prepositional phrases

Possessive prepositional phrases using *of* are quite rare. You wouldn't write 'the baggage of the climbers'; instead, you would write 'the climbers' baggage' using an apostrophe. If there was only one climber, you would put the apostrophe before the s: climber's.

**Answer the following questions.**

1. Which nouns do these adjectival prepositional phrases describe?

   Wilfred Noyce wanted to reach the far stone *further up the mountain*. In 1953, the team reached the top *of the mountain*.

2. Which verbs do these adverbial prepositional phrases describe?

   Unfortunately, these climbers leave litter *on the way*.
   Local sherpas help the climbers *with their baggage*.

3. Are these phrases adjectival or adverbial?

   **a** I gobbled up my snacks *of cockroaches and ants*. Delicious!

   **b** He vaulted over the gate and smiled *with arrogant pride*.

   **c** How dare you answer back *in that rude way*!

4. Imagine you are climbing a mountain or a rock face and you are nearly at the top. Write a brief description of the effort it takes and the moment of triumph when you reach the summit.

   When you have finished, count how many prepositional phrases you have used, and note whether they are adjectival or adverbial.

## Drifting

Every night I am at home in my dreams,
but when the morning breaks,
I must **gallop** back,
back to the realm of eternal ice.

A summer day, 81 degrees north latitude.
It is lovely, a poem of clear white sunbeams
refracted in the **cool crystal blue** of the ice,
so wonderfully calm and still.
Not a sound to be heard
but the drip,
drip,
drip
of water from a block of ice
or the **dull thud**
of a **snow-slip**
from
some hummock.
My thoughts fly free and far
in the profound peace
of the arctic solitude.
Surely the drift
will become faster and faster,
as we get farther Northwest.
Why should not this winter
carry the *Fram*
to someplace north,
north of Franz Josef Land?
Then off I'd fly
with dogs and sledges
to the point where the earth's axis ends.
And the whole
would go
like a dance!

'Drifting' by Bobbi Katz

### Word cloud

cool crystal blue
dull thud
gallop
snow-slip

### Glossary

**realm** a kingdom

**north latitude** in a place north of the equator

**refracted** to bend a ray of light when it enters water or glass

**hummock** a small hill or hump

**the *Fram*** the name of a ship used to explore the Arctic in the nineteenth century

## Understanding

**Answer the following questions.**

1. What sights and sounds does the poem describe?
2. Which lines do you think are the best description of the Arctic? What makes them so effective?
3. How does the narrator feel about the Arctic environment? Which words or phrases in the poem tell you this?
4. How does the narrator feel at the end of the poem? What makes you think this?

## Developing your language – onomatopoeia

*Onomatopoeia* is one of the most difficult words you will ever have to spell. Split it into sections like this: *ono – mato – poeia*.

Now think about the following words and the example meanings given for them.

- *Tear* is the sound you make when you pull a piece of paper apart with the fingers of both hands.
- *Crack* is what happens when a ball hits a window.
- *Split* is the sound you make when you chop a piece of wood in two with an axe.

Read this sentence that shows what running water sounds like.

> The rainwater gurgled down the drainpipe and bubbled over the sidewalk.

**Answer the following questions.**

1. What do you think *onomatopoeia* is? Write a definition.
2. Write one really good example of an onomatopoeic word.

## Word builder

### A word-association game

1. Identify onomatopoeic words and phrases within Drifting (there are some in the Word cloud). Say each one aloud. After you say each one, say another word that you would associate with it.
2. Take each of the words in the Word cloud and think of a scenario to suit it. For example, you might hear snow-slip as snow melts on a frozen playground.

**Key concept**

### Onomatopoeic words

Words used for onomatopoeia are called onomatopoeic words. They usually come from North European languages. Latin and Greek words are longer and rarely imitate the five senses. Onomatopoeic words are often shorter and less grammatically structured than other words with similar meanings. For example, *split* sounds like cutting something in two violently, but *separate*, which has the same dictionary meaning, does not convey this.

## Spelling round-up

Here is a list of 50 words that some people find difficult to spell. Learn them now and you will have far less trouble in the future.

accommodation argument audience beginning believe business conscience conscious
continuous decision definite development disappear disappoint embarrass environment
finally government happened imaginary interesting interrupt knowledge lonely lovely
medicine miscellaneous mischievous necessary original parallel peaceful people
permanent possession preparation receive reference remember safety secretary
separate sincerely skilful successful surprise tomorrow unfortunately weird women

## Speaking, listening – and spelling

### The stickperson spelling competition

Choose a student to be the speller. The speller reads out a word from the list above and everyone writes what they think is the right spelling. The speller reads out the correct spelling and the students who got it right draw one of following on their stickperson: a hand, a foot, an eye, the nose, or the mouth. Change to a new speller and a new word. The first person to complete the stickperson (with eight correct spellings) is the winner and starts the next competition as speller.

### A disease called spellaemia

Once upon a time there was a person called Mr Loudmouth, who was a marvellous speller and liked to show off to his friends. One day he caught a nasty virus that had some peculiar effects, such as making him walk backwards and spell words in a most odd way.

He was very distressed, so his friends took him to see Dr Spell, the famous virologist. The doctor gave Mr Loudmouth some horrid medicine, which sort of cured him. But when he got home he had forgotten how to spell, so his friends had to teach him again. Luckily, it did not take too long and he was soon showing off again.

Present this story as a short drama, making it as funny as you can. Make Mr Loudmouth into a bossy character. Use some of the 50 words in the spelling list – and learn the spellings as you go.

## Solving anagrams

1. These are anagrams of some of the 50 words in the spelling list. Solve each one and write down the word it makes (making sure you spell the word correctly).

| | | | |
|---|---|---|---|
| ever ice | eel pop | it's entering | i voices hums |
| scout union | seen cry | airing yam | fine diet |
| repeat as | appraised | | |

2. Now create six anagrams of your own by using some of the other words in the 50-word spelling list.

**Remember**

An **anagram** is made when you jumble up the letters in a word or words. For example, *sword* is an anagram of *words*.

## Proofreading

You probably spend time reading your own work carefully to see whether you have made any mistakes that need correcting. Today you are going to pretend you are the teacher and you are reading someone else's work. Find the mistakes and write the corrections out. You should recognise some of the misspelt words! These words have been selected because they can be difficult to spell. They are worth learning because you will almost certainly use most of them in your writing.

I was standing on the bridge enjoying the lovley evening and the peacefull atmosphere. Suddenly my thoughts were interupted by the sound of a train in the distance. I was concious that it was approaching fast by its continous roar and the clank of the metal wheels on the rails. Then its lights were upon me as it made the bridge shudder and shake, shattering the safty of my little enviroment. A few seconds later it dissapeared into the distance. Somehow I felt very lonley.

## Content and language in poetry

Listen to a group of students making decisions about the content and language of a poem they are writing together.

**Word cloud**

| | |
|---|---|
| destroyed | strands |
| races | strapped |
| rushing | trudge |

## Understanding

**Answer the following questions about the dialogue you have heard.**

1. For their topic the students chose their journey to school over an old rope bridge. Give two reasons why they have to take that route.
2. Why did they think the bridge was horrid?
3. How do you know the bags of books on the students' backs were heavy?
4. How far above the river was the bridge?
5. Explain how you know that the ropes were very thin.
6. There was not time for the class to decide on a title for the poem. Can you think of a suitable title?

### Glossary

**"cos"** short form of *because* used in talking to each other

**"yeah, cool"** in this context: "Yes, I like it"

**"over to you"** it's your turn now

**"you've got it"** you've understood

**"brilliant"** very well done

**"cheeky"** rude, but not seriously so

## Word builder

Write a mini saga using the words *destroyed*, *rushing*, *strands*, *strapped*, and *trudged*. The task is to write a maximum of 50 words, so you'll need to work hard to keep to the point and make your mini saga flow smoothly, as well as engage your reader.

Here's how you might start:

> My friend and I were at the local river boat races and, although we were strapped in together,...

However, you might prefer to use your own idea.

### Key concept

**Choosing language**

Writers choose their words carefully. If they want to write about something loud and powerful, they use words that make loud and powerful sounds. If they want to write about something soothing and quiet, they use soft words with lots of *m*, *n*, and *l* sounds.

## Developing your language – words that sound hard and powerful

Look again at the words in the Word cloud. Most of them have the letters *t* and *s*. Say these letters aloud with as much emphasis as you can.

All of the words in the Word cloud have an *r* sound. Say this several times with a roaring sound and, if possible, roll the *r* sound.

Now practise saying: *d*, *p*, *sh*, *ch*, *b* and *bl* by reading this tongue-twister aloud. Say it slowly at first then as quickly as you dare.

> To sit in solemn silence in a dull, dark dock,
> In a pestilential prison with a life-long lock,
> Awaiting the sensation of a short, sharp shock,
> From a cheap and chippy chopper on a big, black block.

### Remember

A haiku is a poem with three lines. The first line has five syllables, the second has seven syllables, and the third has five syllables.

**Answer the following questions.**

1. Which letters other than the ones you have practised make a powerful sound, sometimes like an explosion in your mouth?
2. Write two lines of a poem, with a rhyme if possible, to describe a thunderstorm right over your head.
3. Write a haiku about a huge waterfall.
4. Write a mini saga about someone who could not stand the noise in a hot factory full of old-fashioned machines. Describe what the person did. Use words that sound hard to describe the factory.

When you have finished your writing, read it aloud, making the hard-sounding words as powerful as you can.

## Writing about a poem you like

This is your chance to choose a poem you like and to write about it. With a partner, read this conversation aloud.

Student 1: Well, I've chosen my poem. Now how do I start?

Student 2: You need to tell your reader what it's about. Write a quick summary of the content of the poem in not more than about five lines. Then say what you think the most important or interesting part of the poem is.

Student 1: Then there's the title of the poem. It might be a good idea to explain why I think it is called that.

Student 2: Good idea. That's all you need for the first part. Now you need to describe what the poem looks like on the page – I mean whether it is in verses, the lines are short or long, whether there are rhymes – this helps you to know whether it is a serious or a light-hearted sort of poem.

Student 1: I'd like to write about the words the writer uses to describe things – words I like the sound of or that have extra layers of meaning – words that help me to see and hear what the writer is describing.

Student 2: Good idea. There are all those things such as alliteration, similes, metaphors, and onomatopoeia that we've learned about – tricks that writers have with words. You can write some of them down and then explain why you've chosen them.

Student 1: Yes, anything like that. I'll have to choose because there won't be room for everything. Now, for the last part of my writing, I'd like to explain why I like the poem and what my favourite line is, perhaps.

Student 2: So, there we have it. Three parts – first, what the poem is about, second, how it is written, and third, why you have chosen it.

## Writing about a poem

Here is a student's response to 'Drifting'. Notice how each section of this response includes some quotations from the poem to support the student's ideas.

### What the poem is about

This poem is about an explorer in the Arctic. His boat is stuck in the ice, surrounded by the calm, frozen ocean. I think the most important part is at the end when he gets excited by the thought of reaching the North Pole, which is 'the point where the earth's axis ends.' It's called 'Drifting' because the explorer realizes that his boat is drifting very slowly northwards in the frozen ocean. The title also reflects the explorer's thoughts drifting, which I think is great – like a double meaning.

### How the poem is written

This poem is broken up, but not into evenly sized verses. The lines are of different lengths, which I think reflects thoughts flying free and far. If the lines were even lengths, it might feel less exciting. The words are the most important things about the poem. They are often quite simple, but they describe the 'calm and still' environment very clearly. As well as onomatopoeia, the poet uses alliteration. The 'c' sounds in 'cool crystal' make me think of ice.

### Why I have chosen to write about this poem

I chose this poem because I like to read about explorers and history. It must have been so exciting to discover an unknown place! I think you get a really good idea of the explorer's excitement, as well as the peacefulness of the Arctic. The choice of words is great.

My favourite lines are:

'Not a sound to be heard
but the drip,
drip
drip
of water from a block of ice'

The poet uses the repeated word 'drip' to help you imagine the water dripping slowly and quietly from the melting ice.

Now choose a poem yourself and write about it using the headings in the boxes above.

## Progress check

1. How long do you think a journey is? Give a reason for your answer. [2 marks]
2. What two things do you think were unique about how the poem 'Breathless' came to be written? [2 marks]
3. What is proofreading and why is it important? [2 marks]
4. What are two important things about a mini saga? [2 marks]
5. 'There was much rejoicing when the climbers arrived at the summit.' In this sentence *at the summit* is a prepositional phrase. Which word is the preposition and is this an adjectival or an adverbial phrase? [2 marks]
6. Which language group do onomatopoeic words come from? Why is this group best suited to imitate the meanings of words by their sounds? Give two examples of onomatopoeic words. [4 marks]
7. Suggest four things that made the climb described in 'Breathless' very difficult for Wilfred Noyce. [4 marks]
8. In 'Drifting' we learn about the stillness of the Arctic. Find four movement words in the poem which contrast with this idea of stillness. [4 marks]
9. When you write about a poem, what should you include? Name at least four things. [4 marks]
10. When the teacher in the recording wanted her students to write a poem together, how did she make this happen? Name at least four things she did. [4 marks]

## Reflecting on your learning

### Writing about a poem

**Choosing a poem**

I find choosing a poem easy. ☐
I find choosing a poem fairly easy. ☐
I need help choosing poems. ☐

**Summarising the meaning**

I find this easy. ☐
Some meanings cause me difficulty. ☐
I need help to summarise meanings. ☐

**Lines and verses**

I understand why writers choose the shape they use. ☐
I can understand some of the obvious reasons for writers' choices about lines and verses. ☐
I can see why they make their choices once someone explains it. ☐

**Power words**

I see why writers choose particular words. ☐
I can sometimes see why particular words are chosen. ☐
I can see why particular words are chosen once someone explains it. ☐

**Expressing a preference**

I have reasons and quotations to prove them. ☐
I have reasons but cannot use quotations very well. ☐
I need help in expressing my reasons and in using quotations. ☐

**Focus on the areas you need to improve. Ask yourself these questions.**

- Now that I have tried writing about a poem, what did I find difficult and will have to work at?
- How can I work at the parts I found difficult, and what do I want to do better in just a few weeks' time?
- When I've done this work, how will I know that I am getting better at writing about poems?

# 7 Heroic history

In this unit you will:

**Explore**
- a legend from the land of the Cherokee Indians
- a strange hall at the bottom of a lake

**Create**
- an undersea adventure
- your own myth or legend

**Engage**
- with tales that are precious to people's culture
- with the past before stories were written down

**Collaborate**
- in an interview with a hero
- in planning a guide book for an old castle

**Reflect**
- on the fear caused by strange and monstrous creatures
- on the great deeds of heroes

A hero rides out

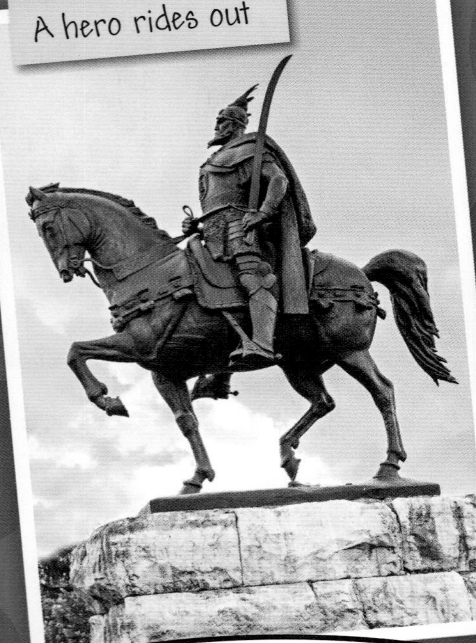

Beowulf fights with the dragon

Myths and legends are all very well: I like real facts!

Heroes are the stuff of legends and they make you feel good.

I can't remember what I did last week, so why do we read about things that are so old we can't even put a date on them?

7

## Thinking time

1. Look at the pictures on the opposite page. Discuss whether they match your idea of a hero.
2. How would you answer the person who said he liked 'real facts'?
3. Why do you think it is important to look back in time as far as is possible?
4. Think of a fourth quote about heroes.

## Speaking and listening

This unit takes you back into the mists of time. There have always been heroes, both men and women, who saved lives and sometimes whole nations. This activity is to make you think about modern heroes.

Heroes in films and on television can sometimes be make-believe characters, such as Spiderman or Batman, who have special powers that entertain us. Heroes in sport are the winners who, for example, save a team from defeat.

Heroes in real life save people from fires, floods, and other dangers. Other people who look after you and do things for you, such as your mum and dad, can also be seen as heroes.

**Choose a hero and plan an interview.**

1. Choose a hero to interview for a television programme.
2. You will ask the hero five questions. You can use one of the sets of three questions below, adding two questions of your own, or you can think of five questions of your own.

**a**
- Can you tell me about yourself?
- What exactly happened?
- What did you think at the time and how do you feel now?

**b**
- Do/did you like playing that character?
- What was your favourite moment in the film?
- What do you say if someone recognises you in the street?

**c**
- Did you always want to have a family?
- What are your favourite moments with us kids?
- Do you sometimes get fed up?

Encourage the person you are interviewing to explain his or her answers.

## 'The Legend of Catahecassa and the Two-horned Snake'

In times when **legends** were told round firesides, **tradition** has it that the Cherokee Indians were plagued by monstrous and menacing snakes. These yellow or orange striped snakes shone as brightly as sunbeams and had two pointed horns upon their heads. Your eyes were drawn to them. Horned snakes had magical powers of magnetism. Try to escape and you were dragged back towards their fangs. They were exceedingly difficult to kill, though the Cherokees believed a skilled marksman might succeed by planting an arrow into the snake's seventh stripe.

One day, the **account** continues, the Cherokees captured a Shawnee youth called Catahecassa. Jokingly, they offered him freedom if he destroyed a horned snake. Accepting the challenge, Catahecassa set off, climbing mountains, clambering through caves, confident that he would encounter a dreaded snake.

And so he did. High among the crags, he sensed something that slithered and slid. Suddenly he saw two horns that led him to his prey. He hurriedly built a circle of pine cones, which he lit. He approached the snake as silently as midnight and slowly raised his bow. The snake glimpsed him – but too late. The arrow sped towards the seventh stripe of the snake's skin. Catahecassa leapt into the ring of fire, avoiding the poison that flowed like a **torrent** from the dying body.

Catahecassa was freed and he became a hero.

The **myth** of the two-horned snake lived on through the ages.

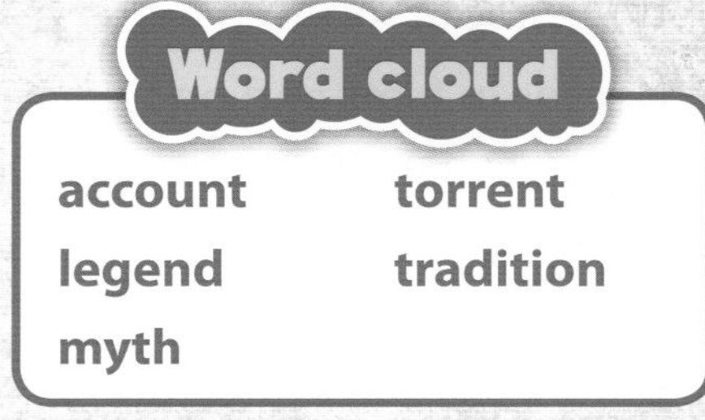

planting an arrow

unerringly

lived on through the ages

## Understanding

**Answer the following questions.** Some questions have more than one answer.

1. Based on this legend's description, what are the other features of a two-horned snake?
2. Why would the snake be dangerous, even when it lay dying?
3. How does the writer create an atmosphere of magic in this legend?

**Key concept**

**Alliteration**

The sound of the words is made more effective by using alliteration, for example 'magical powers of magnetism' and 'seventh stripe of the snake's skin'.

4. What suggests that Catahecassa was brave and sensible?
5. Can you think of any other words to describe him?
6. Why do you think the story says *jokingly* to describe the Cherokees offering Catahecassa his freedom?

## Developing your language – using similes

A simile is when you say that something is like something else. You do this to give the reader a better idea of what you want to say. You can link your simile to the sentence with *like* or *as*.

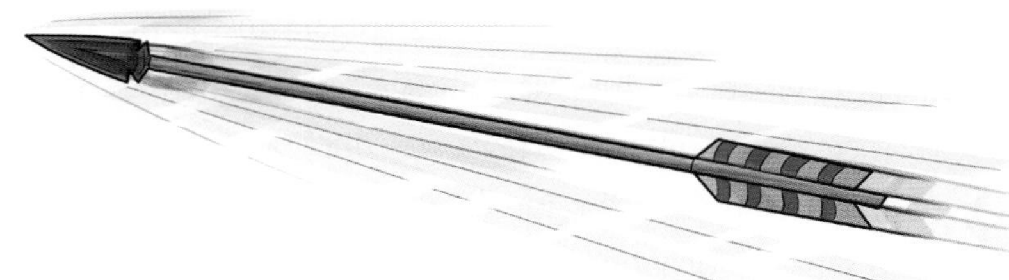

An example from 'The Legend of Catahecassa and the Two-horned Snake' is the phrase that says two-horned snakes 'shone as brightly as sunbeams'. Sunbeams are so bright that sometimes you must wear dark glasses to look at them, so the simile tells you the two-horned snakes were extremely bright.

**Answer the following questions.**

1. What simile could you use for 'the arrow sped like...'?
2. What simile could you use for 'the stripes on the snake's body were like...'?
3. Explain the connection between your simile and the arrow, then your simile and the stripes.

Key concept

**Similes**

Use similes in your stories and descriptions sparingly. Always make sure they add something to what you describe – they are not just for decoration!

## Word builder

Three similes are used in 'The Legend of Catahecassa and the Two-Horned Snake': 'as brightly as sunbeams' (lines 3-4); 'as silently as midnight' (line 19); and 'flowed like a torrent' (line 22).

Read each sentence below and say why a simile would give a better picture. Then change each sentence so it includes a simile.

The snake's head gleamed very brightly.

The two horns led him straight to his prey.

He approached the snake very silently.

The snakes shone, reflecting the light.

Catahecassa set off in a hurry, climbing mountains.

like a

## Paragraph building

Nearly everything you read and write is put into paragraphs because it needs to be in order. Otherwise you would be very confused.

Here is the opening paragraph from a story called 'The Legend of the Old Lady of the Woods', with the sentences jumbled up. Each sentence has been numbered.

> 1. This was because the dragon was subject to the old lady's powers. 2. Whenever they were ill she tended them as though she were their own mother. 3. There was once a very old, wise lady who lived in the depths of the jungle. 4. She also protected travellers from a massive dragon that inhabited the highest branches of the trees. 5. She loved the animals that visited her rundown dwelling.

**Carry out the following activity and answer the questions.**

**1.** In groups, stand in a line. Each person reads one of sentences aloud. Move around until the sentences are in the best possible order. Read the reordered paragraph aloud. Discuss what you did.

**2.** **a** Which words helped you to decide which was the first sentence in the story?

**b** How did the word *whenever* help you to decide which two sentences were next to each other?

**c** How did using *also* help you to decide the order?

**d** How else did you work out the order of the sentences?

**e** Look carefully at the picture of the old lady.

Write a short paragraph to describe the old lady as precisely as you can. Before you start, decide:

- how many sentences you will need
- what the order of your sentences will be.

**Remember**

A paragraph is a group of sentences all on the same topic. It isn't just one sentence, and the sentences are not in a random order.

Here are some starting points you could use for your sentences:

- The first thing I noticed...
- It was cold so the old lady wore...
- Despite the hardships of her life,...
- To sum up, this lady...

## Building more paragraphs

**Answer the following questions.**

1. Look carefully at the tumbledown dwelling where the old lady of the woods lived.

   Make up a sentence to describe something about the dwelling and the place where it was built.

   In groups, say your sentences. Move around until you have an orderly paragraph. The first sentence may have to be changed so that it introduces the paragraph.

2. Now you are going to build two paragraphs in which you discuss whether living in a dwelling like this would be a bad thing or a good thing for you. Before you start, discuss the inconveniences and hardships of living there. Then think of some reasons why someone may like to live there – or go there for holidays.

   When you build your paragraphs, remember to explain your reasons and not just list them.

   In your first paragraph you will need a good way to introduce your ideas, for example:

   To live in a dwelling like this would be hard for me because...

   I do not think I would enjoy...

   Perhaps later you could use discourse markers. A discourse marker is a signpost to where your argument is going next.

   Another reason that I would not want to...

   As the dwelling is in such a remote location,...

   The dwelling looks very insecure, so...

   You could start your second paragraph like this:

   On the other hand,...

   However, there may be some advantages...

   Later you may say:

   Since I love animals,...

   However, my chief reason...

   You could end with:

   Therefore, on balance, I have decided...

   To sum up, ...

**Key concept**

### Discourse markers

These words and phrases are called discourse markers because they mark stages along an argument. Using them will make your paragraphs clearer and more orderly.

## 'Beowulf, the Mighty Hero'

Beowulf was a legendary Danish hero who saved the royal court from a terrible monster called Grendel. However, Grendel's mother came seeking revenge. Beowulf followed her to her lair under the misty lake.

Beowulf dived into the fathomless water. Weird creatures clutched at him with jagged claws and tore at his armour. Grendel's mother laughed evilly. With a sudden rush, she launched herself upwards and wrapped her arms tightly around Beowulf. Unable to move, he was dragged down.

When he came to, he saw that he stood in a **cavernous** hall with a roof of **stout** wooden rafters. Beneath his feet were **glassy** tiles. He could hear distant sounds of the lake above, but the hall was completely dry. The **nightmarish** flames of a **colossal** fire cast **unearthly shadows** on the walls. Then he saw a shape of a giant, towering above him like a great mountain. It was Grendel's mother.

With bare hands he wrestled with this monster, tearing at her hair, but she was too powerful for him by far. She pinned him down and, maddened with her desire for revenge, drew a sharp knife and struck at him.

It should have been the end. Beowulf would have died ignominiously at the bottom of the lake in the monster's cavern. Instead, his armour saved him and the knife was blunted. A tremendous sword, so massive that only a giant could have owned it, hung on the wall. With a superhuman effort Beowulf seized it, swung round, and with one stroke felled the monster stone dead.

### Word cloud

| | |
|---|---|
| cavernous | shadows |
| colossal | stout |
| glassy | unearthly |
| nightmarish | |

### Looking closely

when he came to

by far

pinned him down

stone dead

## Understanding

**Answer the following questions.**

1. How did Grendel's mother try to kill Beowulf?
2. What two things suggest that Beowulf was outstandingly strong?
3. Where is the turning point in the story?
4. What makes the story exciting?

### Remember

Coordinated sentences, such as the one that begins 'With a superhuman effort' (line 22), can have more than two phrases or clauses. You don't have to put *and* between each one, just between the last two.

## Developing your language – different sorts of adjectives

The examples of adjectives listed opposite come from 'Beowulf, the Mighty Hero'. When you write you may want to use the nouns given, or the corresponding adjective may be a better choice. For example, you could write 'at the bottom of the lake there was a great cavern', or you may prefer 'the space between the rocks was cavernous'.

**Answer the following questions.**

1. What did you notice about the spelling of *spacious*, *menacing* and *powerful*?
2. How do these words help to create a frightening image of what was under the lake?

## Word builder

The words in the Word cloud help to build an image of the hall under the lake. For each example below, write your own Word cloud, starting with the words given then listing your own words to achieve the aim. Use a thesaurus to help you.

1. Start with *cavernous* and *colossal*. Aim: to describe how big the hall is.
2. Start with *nightmarish* and *shadows*. Aim: to describe the frightening effect of the fire in the hall.
3. Start with *stout*. Aim: to describe the strength of the beams and the walls.
4. Start with *glassy*. Aim: to describe the appearance of the floor and what it was like to walk on it.

Key concept

### Using adjectives

When you write, you may wish to use a noun or the corresponding adjective may be a better choice.

From 'Beowulf, the Mighty Hero':

cavern – cavernous

fathom – fathomless

power – powerful

tower – towering

lake - lakeside

Other similar examples:

spacious

hopeless

merciful

menacing

riverside

## Developing your language – writing a description

Write a description of a visit to the sea bed. You could include diving downwards and what you see – perhaps coral, or the remains of a wreck.

Practise using the words you have already learnt when you write about what you see and how you feel.

Use some of the words from 'Beowulf, the Mighty Hero' to help you. For example, you could use *fathomless* to express how deep you are diving, or *towering* to describe the size of a wreck.

## Building stories and information texts

Just as the sentences in a paragraph must be in the right order, so must the paragraphs in a longer piece of writing.

**Look carefully at 'Beowulf, the Mighty Hero' and answer these questions.**

1. How many paragraphs are there in the story?
2. How many sentences are there in each paragraph?
3. How do the first two or three words in each paragraph link to the one before?

This is a picture map of the castle grounds that Beowulf may have visited to fight Grendel.

The king lived in the castle, the forest was for hunting for food, the stables were for horses, the lake was full of fish, and the dwellings were where the servants lived.

**Study the map and answer the questions.**

1. Plan a guide book to explain this castle to visitors. Think of each of the five sections of the picture map as a paragraph for the guide book.
2. Decide the following:
   - **a** What will you call the guide book?
   - **b** What order will the five sections appear in?
   - **c** Can you think of a good sentence to start the guide book?
   - **d** Visitors to the castle will want to walk from one feature to another, using your book. How will you link one paragraph to another?
3. Choose one of the sections of the picture map. List the information you can give about it in your guide book. For example, some of the things you may list about the lake are: where it is; how long it is; whether it can be used for fishing; whether you can swim in it safely.
4. Give a brief talk, using your list of information, and listen to others talking about different sections of the guide book.

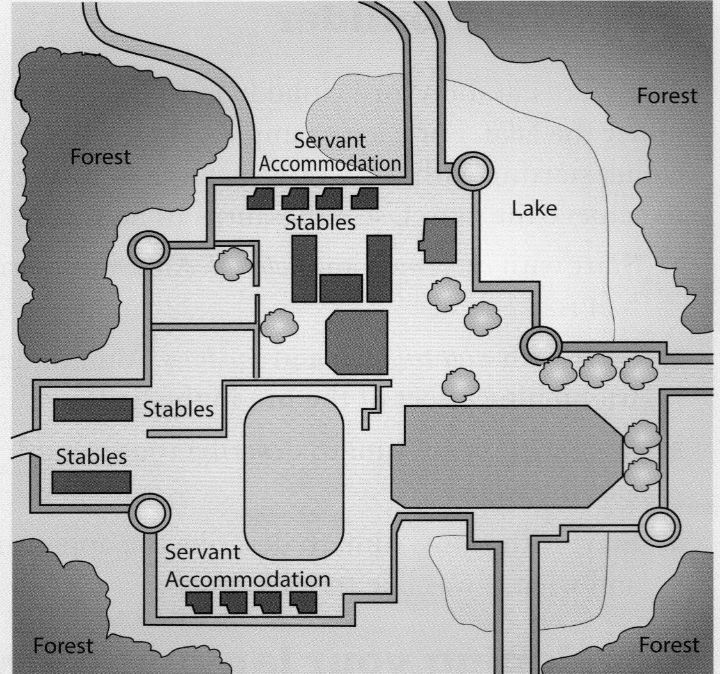


**Key concept**

### Writing paragraphs

Paragraphs can be of different lengths. Use short paragraphs for special effects. In your longer stories or, for example, when presenting an argument or factual information, you will write four, five, or six paragraphs.

## Connectives as discourse markers

There are many words and phrases you can use at the beginnings of paragraphs that serve as connectives. Some of these connectives are also discourse markers.

If you are writing about life at the castle, you may start a new paragraph with expressions such as:

Another feature of daily life was...

However, life was not easy for a servant at the court.

Consequently, the seasons played an important part in life at the court.

As the king spent so much time away from his castle,...

So that food was always available,...

Imagine the last line of your first paragraph mentions servants' comfortable lives. *However* is a signpost that tells readers that the next paragraph will make a contrasting point.

Discuss what the following words tell you and how each example could link to the paragraph before: *consequently*, *because*, and *so that*.

When you write arguments or give information, you may want to change the direction of what you are saying. You can use discourse markers when you write or speak to express:

- purpose – *so that*, *in order to*, *so as to*
- reason – *because (of)*, *since*, *as*, *owing to*
- result – *as a result*, *therefore*, *consequently*
- contrast – *but*, *however*, *in spite of*, *nevertheless*, *although*
- time – *when*, *after(wards)*, *until*, *before*
- place – *where*, *wherever*.

My parents went out shopping. Therefore I was left alone in the house.

In the above example, *therefore* is a discourse marker and tells you the result of other things that happened.

**Complete these sentences using discourse markers from the list above.**

1. ... of the incidence of malaria, we have to take special precautions.
2. ... my family does not have a great deal of money, we always seem to enjoy ourselves.
3. My homework was all wrong. ... I had to stay in at lunchtime to do it again.
4. ... it was never the same again. The quarrel spoilt everything.

**Remember**

A discourse marker is a word that shows a new direction in an argument.

**Key concept**

### Using connectives

You can use connectives to change the direction of what you are writing or saying. Sometimes these connectives come at the beginnings of paragraphs and link ideas from one paragraph to another. You can also use them anywhere to show results, reasons, purposes, and contrasts, and they are referred to as discourse markers.

## Should myths and legends be in history or English lessons?

## Understanding

In this recording you will hear three people, a girl (Sylvanella), her brother (Kefentse), and their mother (Mma Olebetse) who is passing in and out of the room.

**Listen to the recording and answer these questions.**

1. What three things did Mma Olebetse say she had mislaid during the recording?
2. Why did Sylvanella say 'coincidence' near the beginning of the recording?
3. Aesop's fables have morals at the end of them. What is a moral?
4. What ideas did you hear in the recording that suggest myths and legends have some links with history?
5. Which side of the debate do you agree with and why?

### Word cloud

ancient
classical
old-fashioned
primitive
senility
time-honoured

### Looking closely

don't they go better?
folk memory
cheeky
look at the time!

## Developing your language – definitions

The words in the Word cloud are all associated with *old*. Some more examples are *old-fashioned*, *antique*, *antediluvian*, *obsolete*, *venerable*, and *traditional*.

You can easily use these words in the wrong context. For example, it is correct to say, 'Her house was full of old-fashioned furniture'. It would be wrong to say, 'Greek culture is old-fashioned.' In this context *classical* is the correct word to use.

**Answer the following questions.**

1. Use a dictionary to find the meanings of *antique*, *antediluvian*, and *traditional*.
2. Write your own definition of *hot*:
   - **a** when it is a hot day
   - **b** when it is a spicy meal.
3. Write your own definitions of *doctor*, *teacher*, and *professor*.

**Remember**

A definition is the exact meaning of a word. To define a word precisely you may need several words. The dictionary may also give more than one meaning.

## Word builder

Read each pair of sentences and discuss which sentence uses the word from the Word cloud most appropriately.

1. **a** I enjoy reading about the Egyptians and other ancient civilisations.
   **b** I planted this bush last year so it is ancient.
2. **a** I've just written a classical story about my grandmother.
   **b** I've just read a story about a classical hero called Hercules.
3. **a** Senility caused this tree to fall down.
   **b** This poor old man is confused owing to his senility.
4. **a** My aunt is time-honoured – it is her 50th birthday.
   **b** It is a time-honoured custom to celebrate the first day of spring.

## Developing your language – writing a description

Write a description of this happy couple and their house. Practise using the words you have already learnt that describe old objects and people. Here are some more words that will help you:

- *tumble-down*, *dilapidated*, *ruinous*, *crumbling*, *falling to pieces*
- *elderly*, *pensioners*, *grandparents*, *octogenarians*.

## My superhero legend

Superheroes do not just exist in the past. Discuss some of those you have seen in films and on television. You may have your own fictitious superhero in your culture.

You are going to write a story about a superhero who carries out a daring deed and does good for someone or for many people.

*Superheroes on missions*

## Planning your story

You can write your own version of a story you know, or make up a new one. You may want to write notes, or you may prefer to plan the story in your head – but it is a good idea to have some idea of how your story will end when you start to write. Think about these points:

- Who is your hero? How you would describe this person?
- Is your hero male or female? Does he or she have a helper?
- What does your hero look like and what does he or she wear?
- Is your hero normal in real life, becoming different when he or she is on a mission?
- You need an event – what leads up to it, where does it happen, and how will you make it really exciting?
- How will your superhero react to the event? How will he or she overcome evil?
- How will your story end?

Once you know what you are going to write, think about the words you could use to make the descriptions come to life. You may describe your superhero as *valiant*, *athletic*, *vigorous*, *striking*, *rugged*, *robust*, *muscular*, or *handsome*.

*Fight*, *fall*, and *shout* are over-used words and your writing will be less interesting if you use them. Use your thesaurus to find alternative words. For example:

- instead of *fight* use *grapple*, *come to blows*, *wrestle*, *struggle*, *battle*, *tussle*
- instead of *fall* use *tumble*, *topple*, *trip*, *stumble*, *collapse*, *overbalance*, *stagger*
- instead of *shout* use *yell*, *roar*, *bellow*, *howl*, *exclaim*.

## Structuring your story

The plan below shows how you can set out the content of your story. Suggestions for the first sentences in each paragraph are given, to show how you could link ideas in different paragraphs. Remember to choose your own words.

### The first paragraph

Introduce the place and the big problem. Write a possible first sentence, something like: 'The atmosphere in the town of… was one of great fear…'

### The second paragraph

Now get your story moving with an event and introduce your superhero. You will need a sentence that connects to the first paragraph, something like: 'One day that will always be remembered, a most terrible thing happened…'

### The third paragraph

This is the exciting part of the story, where the superhero tries to solve the problem and is almost overcome by an evil force. You will need your powers of description in this paragraph. Your first sentence needs to keep the story moving, something like: 'Suddenly, the people in the square caught sight of a brightly coloured figure climbing up the outside of the building…'

### The fourth paragraph

This is the turning point of the story. Your superhero is in a peril and something must happen to bring good fortune and to solve the problem. It is in this paragraph that your superhero succeeds in the mission. Your opening sentence could connect to the third paragraph, something like: 'At long last,… opened his (or her) eyes and saw an amazing sight…'

### The final paragraph

This is the final, triumphant moment. Describe the celebrations and how people congratulate your superhero. Choose an opening sentence that sums up everything that has gone before, something like: 'Imagine the cheering and waving that greeted…'

## Progress check

1. What are legends and myths? In your definitions, try to suggest a difference between the two. [2 marks]
2. Give the name of someone, male or female, you think is a hero and give a reason for your answer. [2 marks]
3. When Beowulf dived to the bottom of the lake, what two things do you think made his descent very dangerous for him? [2 marks]
4. Can you remember the names of the two tribes of North American Indians named in 'The Legend of Catahecassa and the Two-horned Snake?' [2 marks]
5. What is the difference between a debate and a conversation? [2 marks]
6. How are dragons regarded differently in different parts of the world? Create a sentence with a simile to describe each type of dragon. [4 marks]
7. 'Beowulf, the Mighty Hero' is a good read, but surely no one would believe it is a true story? Give four reasons why you think it cannot be true. [4 marks]
8. What four things do you know about paragraphs? [4 marks]
9. Here are four discourse markers: *because*, *therefore*, *so that*, and *although*. What is each one an example of? [4 marks]
10. Think about any story that goes from beginning to end in four paragraphs. What would you expect to find in each of the paragraphs? [4 marks]

# Reflecting on your learning

## Reading stories

How easy do you find it to read a story from the beginning to the end and to remember what you have read?

When I start to read:

- [ ] I usually get involved very quickly.
- [ ] Whether I get involved quickly depends on what the story is about.
- [ ] I need encouragement to finish.

As I read on:

- [ ] I read steadily and confidently.
- [ ] I sometimes have to go back over what I have read.
- [ ] I read slowly.

As I get near the end:

- [ ] I remember what has happened and get involved with the characters.
- [ ] I remember the gist but the details escape me.
- [ ] I can talk about the story with help.

When I get to the end:

- [ ] I have read the story quickly and efficiently.
- [ ] I think maybe I read too quickly and missed some detail.
- [ ] I may not remember everything but it feels like a huge achievement to have finished!

**Focus on the areas you need to improve. Answer these questions.**

- What can I do now to improve the ways in which I go about reading stories?
- What could I do in the longer term to help me:
  - increase my desire to read
  - choose which stories to read
  - train myself to respond to what I have read?
- How will I know when I have improved the speed at which I read and my understanding of what I have read?

# 8 Exciting escapades

In this unit you will:

**Explore**
- how writers 'hook' readers with their story openings
- how to create vivid characters in writing

**Create**
- a presentation about books and reading
- an exciting adventure story

**Engage**
- with an extract from a novel by Khaled Hosseini
- with writing 'flash fiction'

**Collaborate**
- to explore different ways of structuring stories
- to play the adverb game

**Reflect**
- on which books and authors you enjoy reading
- on the importance of 'show not tell' in writing

'Whenever you read a good book, somewhere in the world a door opens to allow in more light.'
Vera Nazarian

'Write the kind of story you would like to read. People will give you all kinds of advice about your writing, but if you are not writing something you like, no one else will like it either.'
Meg Cabot

'You know you have read a good book when you turn the last page and feel a little as if you have lost a friend.'
Paul Sweeney

## Thinking time

1. What books and stories do you enjoy reading? What is your favourite book of all time?
2. In your opinion, what makes a good book?
3. What type of stories do you enjoy writing? If it's different from what you enjoy reading, why is this?
4. What do you enjoy about writing stories?
5. Have you written a story that you are particularly proud of?
6. What is the hardest thing about writing a story?

## Speaking and listening

Write a presentation recommending books, stories, and poems for 10–12 year olds.

In your presentation:

- say why reading is important and enjoyable
- give the title and author of each book, story, or poem
- sum each up in 1 sentence.

## Choosing a good book

Interesting plot and great characters; you sort of like the bad guy even though you know he shouldn't be telling lies. It made me think about the choices the hero and heroine make as well.

The other two are pretty good as well. The writer of the mystery keeps you guessing to the end and The Mustang in the Canyon is nothing like a girlie pony story. It's set in Wyoming; you can almost feel the wind and see the amazing landscape. The author actually made me want to cry, but don't tell anyone

**Answer these questions and explain your opinions.**

1. What is Paula trying to find out?
2. **a** What attitude to reading does Laurent, who first speaks to Paula, have?

   **b** Does Marcus have a different attitude? In what way?
3. Why is Laurent's comment 'boring' not a satisfactory answer?
4. Why are Marcus's answers more useful to Paula?

### Remember

Think about your audience. Your audience is younger than you, so you need to think about how you are going to make your presentation interesting and entertaining for them.

# Tribes

**Read the story opening below.**

'He must be here somewhere!'

Kevin Davidson held his breath and pressed himself against the wall of the derelict shop. He tried to merge into the grey concrete to make himself invisible. Difficult when you're wearing a red tracksuit.

It didn't work.

'There he is!'

In the twilight, Kevin could just make out the boy with the black hair who was pointing at him. Why did he hate him? Kevin wondered. He had never seen him before, never seen any of them. Yet here they were, like a pack of rabid dogs drooling over him. Kevin threw himself forward and jumped over a broken wall. They broke into a **run** after him. One, two, three – more of them appearing from every direction.

'You can't run from us,' one of them shouted, 'You can't hide.'

They were right. He didn't know this part of town well enough to hide from them. Where could he go? Where was safe?

Nowhere. Not here. Not for him.

He kept running, though his legs were aching and his heart was pounding. It was fear that kept him going. Why were they after him? What had he ever done to them?

He had no doubt that this crowd meant to do some serious kicking if they caught him.

But why?

Because he was new in town?

They were closing in on him. He **glanced** behind and almost **yelled** when he saw how close they were. He rounded a corner and found himself heading for the car park underneath one of the tower blocks. May be he could hide himself there. Find a lift, an escape route. Someone to help him.

They were still behind him. He didn't dare look to see how near, but he could hear their feet **pounding** closer. If he didn't find a hiding place in this car park, he was done for.

from *Tribes* by Catherine MacPhail

## Understanding

1. At the start of the extract, where is Kevin trying to hide?
2. Who is speaking in the first sentence of the extract?
3. Give two reasons why it is difficult for Kevin to get away.
4. How does the writer make the setting seem dangerous?
5. **a** What is 'like a pack of rabid dogs drooling over him' an example of?

   **b** What impression do these words create of the boys chasing Kevin?
6. Explain how the writer tries to make this story opening exciting for the reader.

## Word builder

1. Use the extract and a dictionary to find three synonyms for each of the words in the Word cloud.
2. Compare your words with those of another student. Evaluate whether some synonyms are better than others in the context of the extract.

## Developing your language – story openers

Writers aim to 'hook' the reader at the start of a story and make them want to read on.

Some of the techniques that writers use are shown opposite.

1. How does the extract from *Tribes* start? (There is more than one possible answer.)
2. Which techniques are used in the opening lines below?

   **a** 'I know I'm not an ordinary ten-year-old kid.' (*Wonder* by R.J. Palacio)

   **b** 'There are guns and bandits in this story. And supermodels. And there's drought and starvation too. (*Where I belong* by Gillian Cross)

   **c** 'The monster showed up just after midnight. As they do.' (*A Monster Calls* by Patrick Ness)
3. Suggest the genre of book each of these opening lines come from. Explain your answer.
4. Which of these books would you like to read more of and why?

Describe the setting

Introduce character

Address the reader

Go straight into the action

Provide history/background to the story

Include speech/conversation

Reflect on what has happened

Withhold information from the reader

Suggest what the story is going to be about

Key concept

### Adverbs and adverbials

There are adverbs for time (e.g. *today*), place (e.g. *there*), manner (e.g. *quietly*), and degree (e.g. *almost*).

The three most common adverbs in English are *not*, *very*, and *too*.

Many adverbs are formed by adding *–ly* to an adjective, but there are exceptions to this rule. Examples:

- comfortable ⟶ comfortably
- happy ⟶ happily
- enthusiastic ⟶ enthusiastically

Note that adverbs of manner can be compared. Examples:

*more quietly* (comparative) *most quietly* (superlative)

**Remember**

An adverb is a word that modifies a verb, an adjective, or another adverb.

If you want to check whether a word is an adjective, try putting it in front of a noun to see whether it sounds right.

## Forming adverbs

**Answer the following questions.**

1. Turn these adjectives into adverbs:

   a weary
   b horrible
   c attractive
   d energetic
   e logical
   f hungry
   g ravenous
   h necessary
   i recent

2. Identify the adverbs – and whether they are adverbs of time, place, manner, or degree – in the sentences below.

   a Yesterday, Dan and Suki went to a lovely adventure playground in a forest.
   b An extremely large storm cloud loomed threateningly over them.
   c The sea is just over there beyond the hill you can see clearly in the distance.
   d It was a friendly cat and purred very contentedly when Hanna stroked it.
   e The garden was almost completely overgrown and wonderfully wild.
   f At midnight, the owl, perched solemnly on a branch, gave its nightly call in the darkness.

**3.** Identify the adverbs in this extract. Rewrite it, removing some of the adverbs and replacing some with more precise nouns or verbs. You may decide to keep some.

The goat, Mildew, ran very quickly along the path, pausing occasionally to sniff curiously at pieces of rubbish. Leaves and twigs were lying haphazardly on the ground. Aaina walked quite slowly. 'I never wanted to come here anyway!' she had shouted crossly, back at the cottage, before she ran down the path angrily. She had opened the window fiercely and breathed in the damp air hungrily. 'I really don't like it here!' she'd said quietly and grumpily. It was better out here walking aimlessly in the forest. She shouldn't have spoken sharply to her brother yesterday. She felt guilty and turned back towards the cottage. The goat, sensing something was up, ran quickly after her.

## Adverbial phrases

**Answer the following questions.**

**1.** Look at the sentences below and identify the adverbial phrases.

- **a** The children followed the trail into the forest.
- **b** Jon and Zak crept down to the beach.
- **c** Every day, the old man disappeared into his rickety shed.
- **d** They watched the boat disappear with growing unease.
- **e** In silence, the crowd gaped at the huge jellyfish.
- **f** After the storm, Mairi cried like a small child.

**Remember**

An adverbial phrase (sometimes called an 'adverbial') is a group of words that functions like an adverb.

**2.** Add an adverbial phrase to each of the sentences below.

- **a** The dog growled.
- **b** Running, she slipped and fell.
- **c** He shouted to his mum.
- **d** The door slammed.
- **e** The wind blew fiercely.

## Speaking and listening – the adverb game

Work in small groups. One person from each group leaves the room; the rest of the group choose an adverb. The person then returns and has to guess what the adverb is by asking members of the group to carry out actions 'in the manner of the adverb'.

## And the Mountains Echoed

*Abdullah's father has set off across the desert to Kabul to search for work, taking Abdullah's little sister, Pari, with him. Abdullah begs to be allowed to go with them.*

"All right, then. Come," Father said. "But there won't be any crying. You hear me?"

"Yes."

"I'm warning you. I won't have it."

Pari grinned up at Abdullah, and he looked down at her pale eyes and pink round cheeks and grinned back.

From then on, he walked beside the wagon as it jostled along on the **pitted** desert floor, holding Pari's hand. They traded furtive happy glances, brother and sister, but said little for fear of souring Father's mood and spoiling their good fortune. For long stretches they were alone, the three of them, nothing and no one in sight but the **deep** copper gorges and vast sandstone cliffs. The desert unrolled ahead of them, **open** and wide, as though it had been created for them and them alone, the air **still**, blazing hot, the sky high and blue. Rocks shimmered on the cracked floor. The only sounds Abdullah heard were his own breathing and the rhythmic creaking of the wheels as Father pulled the red wagon north.

A while later, they stopped to rest in the shadow of a boulder. With a groan, Father dropped the handle to the ground. He winced as he arched his back, his face raised to the sun.

"How much longer to Kabul?" Abdullah asked.

Father looked down at them. His name was Saboor. He was dark-skinned and had a hard face, angular and bony, nose curved like a desert hawk's beak, eyes set deep in his skull. Father was thin as a reed, but a lifetime of work had made his muscles powerful, tightly wound like rattan strips around the arm of a wicker chair. "Tomorrow afternoon," he said, lifting the cowhide water bag to his lips. "If we make good time." He took a long swallow, his Adam's apple rising and dropping.

"Why didn't `Uncle Nabi drive us?" Abdullah said. "He has a car."

Father rolled his eyes toward him.

"Then we wouldn't have had to walk all this way."

Father didn't say anything.

Extract from *And the Mountains Echoed* by Khaled Hosseini

### Glossary

**rattan** stems of a palm used to make furniture

**traded** exchanged

**souring** making awkward / difficult

**winced** slight movement caused by pain

| | |
|---|---|
| deep | pitted |
| open | still |

## Understanding

**Answer these questions.**

1. How are Abdullah, Pari and their father travelling?
2. How are they carrying their possessions?
3. What do you learn about the relationship between Abdullah and Pari?

   Find evidence to support your answer.
4. What impression do you get of Father from the way he is presented in this extract?

   For each of your ideas, give supporting evidence from the text.

## Word builder

**Look at the words in the Word cloud.** They are adjectives used to describe the landscape.

1. Identify other adjectives used to describe the landscape.
2. Explain how the writer creates an impression of the hugeness and loneliness of the desert.

## Developing your language – creating character

Which of the following techniques does Hosseini use to develop the character of Father?

- description of his physical appearance
- what the other characters say about him
- what he does
- writer's direct comment
- what he says
- how other characters react to him

Are there other techniques the writer uses to develop Father's character?

Write the next section of *And the Mountains Echoed*, in which you develop the character of Father, using some of these techniques.

Remember to plan your writing.

OR Write your own description of a character, perhaps based on someone you know, using some of these techniques.

Key concept

### Relative clauses

Relative clauses are a type of subordinate clause. They describe or explain something that has just been mentioned, using one of the following relative pronouns:

- who
- whose
- which
- where
- whom
- that
- when.

Example: Of all the team sports, the one *that I prefer* is football. This sport, *which I play with my friends*, is extremely popular all over the world.

Sometimes a relative clause can refer to the rest of the sentence rather than a noun or pronoun.

Example: Suzi did not eat her dinner, *which was unusual*.

Two important rules to remember are:

1. The relative clause must go immediately after the noun or pronoun it refers to.
2. 'Who', 'whose', and 'whom' are used for people and 'that' and 'which' are used for things.

**Remember**

A noun is a word that refers to a person, a place, or a thing. A pronoun is a word that can take the place of a noun.

## Using relative clauses

**Answer the following questions.**

1. Identify the relative clauses in the following sentences.
   - **a** Mr Lee was reading us the story that he had told us about.
   - **b** I crept closer and closer to the door, which was swinging in the breeze.
   - **c** The old boat, which had seen many an exciting adventure, set sail again.
   - **d** The head teacher squinted at the boy whom he had summoned to his office.
2. Identify the errors in the following sentences and write each one out correctly.
   - **a** Benji is the person that I planned to play badminton with.
   - **b** They went to the same forest that Mark had been to it.
   - **c** I have a friend whom mother is a children's author.
   - **d** He saw the man who was following Peter who had dark hair.

Key concept

**Restrictive and non-restrictive clauses**

There are two types of clauses:

- restrictive or defining clauses
- non-restrictive or non-defining clauses.

Restrictive clauses identify the person or thing that is being referred to and are vital to the meaning of the sentence. They are not separated from the rest of the sentence by a comma. With restrictive clauses, you can often drop the relative pronoun.

Example: The letter [that] I wrote yesterday was lost.

A non-restrictive clause provides additional information about a noun. They can be taken away from the sentence and it will still make sense. They are separated from the rest of the sentence by commas (or brackets).

Example: The principal, who liked order, was shocked and angry.

**Note**: 'Which' is used for non-restrictive clauses and 'that' for restrictive clauses.

Remember

You can check by seeing whether the sentence makes sense if you remove the relative clause.

## Types of clauses

**Look at the following sentences and explain whether the relative clause in each sentence is restrictive or non-restrictive.**

1. The boy who broke the window is at the door.
2. I went to New York with the girl who is my best friend.
3. The deep sea diver, who had been waiting to dive, finally took the plunge.
4. This is the dog that has been causing so much trouble.
5. The gate, which had been open suddenly, slammed shut.

## Favourite authors

**Write a short piece of writing about your favourite author.** Use the steps below to help you.

1. Carry out research into one of your favourite authors. It could be a novelist, a poet, or any other writer that you particularly like. Make notes as you do your research.
2. Write up your notes into a short piece of writing. Vary your sentences and aim to use at least three examples of relative clauses.
3. If possible, share your piece of writing with a partner, to check each other's relative clauses.

## What makes a good story?

Listen to this discussion between Aalia, Pabla, Aamir, and Haafiz. They are discussing the books they enjoy reading and what makes a good story. Aalia starts the conversation.

## Understanding

1. Which character from the Harry Potter series does Aalia like best?
2. Why do Aalia and Pabla prefer reading a book to seeing a film of a book?
3. What kind of a book do the group agree the Harry Potter books could be described as?
4. What do Haafiz and Pabla disagree about?
5. What are all the different genres of novel the group mentions?
6. What do the group decide makes for a good story?

## Word builder

The words in the Word cloud are associated with books and stories. **Think of any other words from the discussion that you might use to talk about books and stories. Can you add others to this list?**

## Developing your language – show and tell

**Look at the two descriptions below of Edmond, a character from *How I Live Now*, by Meg Rosoff.** Which one is 'showing' and which one is 'telling'? Discuss and explain how the two descriptions differ.

**A** Edmond is 14-years-old but is very different from most teenagers. (...) His hair is very untidy – he has a really bad haircut, which looks awful. He looks trusting and gentle and as though he needs looking after. I think he looks very sweet and easy to love. He insists on picking up my bag even though he is shorter than me and has very skinny arms. He behaves in a very grown up and responsible way. He takes me home.

**B** Now let me tell you what he looks like before I forget because it's not exactly what you'd expect from your average fourteen-year-old what with the (...) hair that looks like he cut it himself with a hatchet in the dead of night, but aside from that he's exactly like some kind of mutt, you know the ones you see at the dog shelter who are kind of hopeful and sweet and put their nose straight into your hand when they meet you with a certain kind of dignity and you know from that second that you're going to take him home? Well that's him. Only he took me home.

I'll take your bag, he said, and even though he's about half a mile shorter than me and has arms about as thick as a dog leg, he grabs my bag (...)

**Remember**

When you are writing, it is always best to 'show not tell'. In other words, don't tell your reader it's a beautiful day; instead, show it through the way you describe a scene or what someone does or thinks.

## Showing not telling

**Complete the tasks below.** Remember to show not tell.

1. **a** Write three sentences about the character above, choosing details and language that present a positive and sympathetic viewpoint.
   **b** Repeat this process with a negative and critical viewpoint.
   **c** Swap your sentences with a partner to read and review each other's work. Discuss how successfully your views have been conveyed through your language.
2. Now write a description of a character hiding in a dark cave, or another scary place, feeling frightened and lonely, without stating directly where he or she is or explaining your character's feelings explicitly.

## Planning and writing stories

In this section you are going to think about ways of adapting the structure of stories to add interest and variety to your writing.

The simplest way of thinking about structure is:

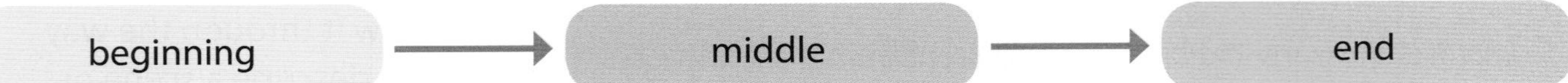


**Think of a well-known story, a fairy story or a fable, and try to tell it in three sentences.** Alternatively, make up your own story, with one sentence for the beginning, one for the middle, and one for the end.

A more detailed structure for a story might look like this:

| **Narrative framework** | |
|---|---|
| Opening | Hooks the reader in/establishes narrative voice/hints at what kind of story it's going to be |
| Description of setting/ development of characters | Builds up a picture of the setting, the characters and the relationship; prepares the reader for problem/complication |
| Problem/complications | Introduces the central event/issue/idea of the story |
| Events | Provides the sequence of events prompted by the problem/ complication |
| Resolution | Resolves or sorts out the problem/complications |
| Reflection | Reflects/thinks about what happened in this story and why, and considers lessons learned or bigger ideas suggested by the story |

Not all stories will include all of these stages. For example, some stories don't have a resolution but end with a cliff hanger, leaving the reader to make up his or her mind about what happened. Sometimes the stages might come in a different order; for example, the story might start in the middle and then include a flashback.

**Think about a story you know – it might be a book you have read in class. How far does it match this structure? Discuss this in a group.**

## Planning the structure of a story

**Carry out the following activity.**

1. In groups, choose a story that you all know well – a fairy tale, a myth, or a legend.
2. Retell the story as a group, with each person telling part of the narrative.
3. Write a plan for the story, dividing it up into five or six sections.
4. Label each section to show which part of the story it is, according to the narrative framework.
5. Discuss how you could adapt the structure of the story; for example, by starting the story in the middle, at the most exciting point, or at the end, reflecting on what has happened.
6. Decide whose point of view you are going to tell the story from. You might want to try an unusual point of view – the perspective of one of the minor characters, for example.
7. Write the first paragraph of your story, remembering the different ways in which you can capture the reader's attention.

## Writing your own story

**Write a story about characters who notice something odd in a deserted house. They decide to investigate.**

Use the ideas and techniques from the rest of this unit, as well as previous units, to help you. Key points to remember:

- the opening should engage the reader immediately
- structure your story to make it interesting for the reader
- include vividly presented characters
- remember to 'show not tell'.

**Remember**

Remember to follow the writing process: plan, draft, edit, proofread.

## Progress check

1. What techniques does Catherine McPhail use to engage the reader in the opening of *Tribes*? [2 marks]
2. Why is the opening of a story or novel so important? [2 marks]
3. Give the three most common adverbs. [3 marks]
4. State the comparative and superlative forms of the adverb *frighteningly*. [2 marks]
5. Explain what an adverbial phrase is and give two examples. [3 marks]
6. Give four examples of adjectives you might use to describe a desert scene and four to describe an Arctic scene. [2 marks]
7. Give two techniques writers use to present characters. [2 marks]
8. What is the difference between a restrictive and non-restrictive relative clause? Give an example of each. [4 marks]
9. What does 'show not tell' mean when you are writing? Give examples to support your answer. [4 marks]
10. List the stages in the narrative framework. Write a short sentence to explain each process. [6 marks]

## Reflecting on your learning

**In pairs, interview each other about your reading and your writing.** The focus of the interview is an opportunity to reflect on what you enjoy and what you feel you are good at, as well as those areas you want to explore and develop further. The interview should be a chance to think about how you felt about the story you wrote at the end of the unit.

Suggested questions:

- What is the book or story you have enjoyed reading most in the last month or so?
- What kinds of books and stories do you enjoy reading generally?
- Could you describe three of your favourite characters from books or stories?
- What books and stories are on your list for reading soon?
- How did you find writing your adventure story?
- Which parts were you most pleased with?
- Were there aspects you were less happy with?

**Copy and complete the following flowchart after your discussion. Monitor your progress against these goals periodically.**

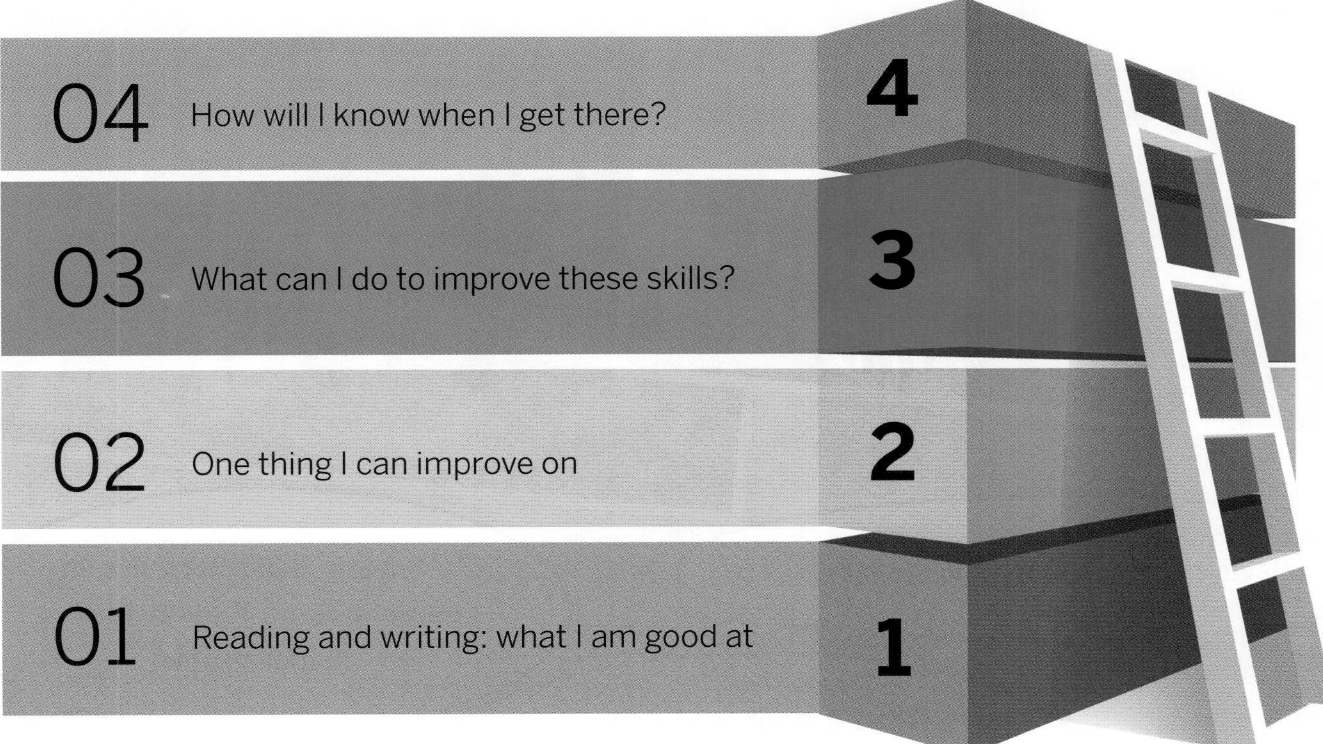

# 9 Tremendous television

**In this unit you will:**

**Explore**
- an African township choir
- the world of international television

**Create**
- an article for a magazine
- two contrasting paragraphs using different sentence lengths

**Engage**
- with a mother's concern about the effect of TV on her children
- with how some young people met with great success

**Collaborate**
- as an audience in a speaking and listening presentation
- to decide on a series of film shots to add to a broadcast

**Reflect**
- on how mums and dads might run a TV station
- on varying language to suit purpose and audience

Television, the great time-waster.

Television characters live in our minds as though they're actual people.

Read a book and your imagination takes over; watch TV and it goes to sleep.

## Thinking time

1. Look at the photos of people watching TV. Which image do you think fits your attitude towards TV and why?
2. Is TV a 'great time-waster'? When and why do you decide something else is more important than watching TV? What actual use do you make of television?
3. What exactly is meant by the reference to our imagination in the second quotation?
4. Look at the third quotation. How can characters become real in this way, and is it true in your experience?
5. Most quotations about TV are very critical. Can you find a quotation or two that gives a reason why we should applaud TV and its programmes?

## Speaking and listening

This is your chance to make a short presentation and to answer questions.

You and many of your friends will probably be in the habit of enjoying the same TV programme each day or week, or you may have watched something different from your friends.

Talk about one or two programmes that you have enjoyed.

Plan what to say and write brief notes – which are not to be read during your presentation!

1. Introduction: 'Today I'm going to talk about a programme that I thought was very ________.'
2. Give a quick summary of what the programme was about.
3. Say what you enjoyed most about the programme: you might mention characters in a drama or a soap; exciting moments in the story; interesting things from a documentary; the way a programme was presented; the background music; or some funny moments in a comedy.
4. Ask your audience for questions and comments (there will be more comments if they watched the same show). Choose who will speak and maybe comment on what they have said.
5. End your presentation by summing up the main points or by looking forward to the next programme in the series.

**Key concept**

### Types of TV programme

A **soap** is a TV serial about everyday lives.

A **documentary** gives factual information about real events.

A **comedy** is a show that makes people laugh.

## Television news – an international miracle

This is a brief article written for an international magazine called *Mothers and Children*.

### TV worldwide!

Most of you probably watched the Olympic Games on television. What exciting moments they provided! Big screens, digital clarity, and bright colours brought the opening and closing ceremonies and the athletes' moments of triumph direct to our homes. We were part of a billion-strong audience, people sharing the same experiences worldwide. Countries with **infinitesimal** numbers of **contestants** held their breath as much as those who competed in every final; national pride was measured in equal proportions whoever we were. We were lucky to be alive!

It wasn't always like that. Not long ago the broadcast quality prevented you from enjoying the **immediacy** of the events. You had to wait until the broadcast was ready for screening in your country and already knew the results. Black and white TV was no fun and before that you relied on radio commentaries to bring you news.

Nowadays, TV is truly international. It brings news as it happens from all corners of the planet. Man. U. becomes a reality and Valtteri Bottas struggles for the podium before your very eyes. You take it for granted, but you are experiencing an outstanding technological wonder.

It doesn't stop there. TV brings to the whole world issues that most concern it. Think about **ecology**. We need to know what happens as we **deplete** the animal kingdom. We need to know the effects of greenhouse gases on the Arctic ice. We need to know about the unsustainable destruction of rain forests. TV brings us news through documentaries. We may not be stirred into action, but at least we are educated. Without TV this does not happen.

TV also allows us to share the world's suffering – warfare, poverty, disease. Commentators travel into the most **inhospitable** parts of the world to report on refugee camps and famine, and we see these for ourselves. We may say, 'Turn off the news – we don't want to know', but we are truly given the chance to see reality.

**Word cloud**

contestants
deplete
ecology
immediacy
infinitesimal
inhospitable

**Glossary**

**held their breath** waited nervously to see what would happen

**no fun** it was not entertaining

**it doesn't stop there** there are yet more arguments to be made

## Understanding

1. Why was the TV coverage of the Olympic Games 'exciting'?
2. Why was TV coverage in the past not as good?
3. Explain carefully in your own words why TV news is much better nowadays.
4. What does the writer mean by 'TV is truly international'?
5. Sum up the main points of the argument in this article, making the writer's attitude towards television clear.

### Looking closely

One of the effects built into this argument is to use the same sentence starter three times to emphasise a point. The writer repeats 'We need to know' on purpose to set up a rhythm in the reader's mind.

## Developing your language – using prefixes

The words in the Word cloud are long. That is because originally they came from Latin and Greek, and because they are made up of different parts you can make more words out of them.

1. Split the word: 'con – test – ants' means 'together – competing – people'.
2. Write a sentence containing this word so that the meaning is clear, like 'All the contestants in the TV quiz show scored at least twenty points.'
3. Look in the dictionary to find other words beginning with 'con–', like 'concert' and 'concentric'. However, you will need to be careful because 'con–' may be confused with another meaning, such as the prefix 'contra'.

In the article 'TV worldwide!' there are some words that use more complicated prefixes.

- What have *documentaries* to do with *documents* and *doctors*?
- What has *digital* to do with *digits* and *digitise*?
- What has *technology* to do with *technician* and *technique*?

### Remember

A **prefix** ('pre–' means 'before') is the beginning of a word made up of different parts (e.g. 'un–', 'de–', or 'con–').

A **suffix** (from 'sub' meaning after/under) is the end part of a word (e.g. '–al', '–able' or '–ise').

## Word builder

**Work together on each of the words in the Word cloud to follow the procedure in 'Developing your language'.**

1. Split each word into its parts, find out what the prefix means, and practise the spelling.
2. Write a sentence to show you understand the meaning of each of the words in the Word cloud.
3. Find at least four other words from the dictionary that start with the same prefix, and practise using them in sentences.

### Key concept

### Spelling using prefixes

Words often come in families, and many words can start with the same prefix, which gives them some common meaning. If you learn to split a complex word into its parts, this can help you with its spelling. You won't be dis–appoint–ed and you will be better at spelling im–mediate–ly.

## Sentence lengths

**1.** Look at these groups of sentences.

> I like watching all sorts of programmes on TV. I think I'm too old for children's TV now. I prefer adventure films and lots of violent fighting. My mother says it isn't any good for me.

> I like watching all sorts of programmes on TV, although I think I'm too old for children's TV now and prefer adventure films and lots of violent fighting, which my mother says isn't any good for me.

> I watch all sorts. I don't like children's TV anymore because I'm simply too old for it and my tastes have changed. I now prefer to watch adventure films with lots of violent fighting. My mum doesn't approve.

**Remember**

An exclamation mark makes a phrase or a short sentence stand out. You usually use it in phrases such as 'How silly I am!' and more freely in dialogue when people are speaking. Don't use it at the end of a long, factual sentence, and don't use it too often.

**2.** Discuss which of the three examples flows best – which do you feel most comfortable with when you read it? Can you work out why?

**3.** Read this extract from 'TV worldwide!'

Most of you probably watched the Olympic Games on television. What exciting moments they provided! Big screens, digital clarity, and bright colours brought the opening and closing ceremonies and the athletes' moments of triumph direct to our homes. We were part of a billion-strong audience, people sharing the same experiences worldwide. Countries with infinitesimal numbers of contestants held their breath as much as those who competed in every final; national pride was measured in equal proportions whoever we were. We were lucky to be alive!

**a** Discuss how many sentences you think there are in this paragraph – be careful.

**b** In the third sentence there is only one verb. What makes it such a long sentence?

**c** The fourth sentence also has one verb, but it is a different type of sentence. How does 'people sharing the same experiences worldwide' relate to the word 'audience'?

**d** Look at the second and the last sentences. Why are they so effective? What effect does the exclamation mark have?

## Writing in different sentence lengths

Practise writing a set of two paragraphs using sentences of different lengths.

Start the first paragraph with 'What a beautiful day!'

Start the second paragraph with 'What a horrible day! I could hardly believe the change in the weather after such a marvellous start to the week.'

## Using questions

Here is another way of talking to your audience when you write.

> The wind was howling like a hungry wolf and the rain was almost horizontal as it drove down our street. The water on the road rippled like an angry river and blew into fantastic shapes. Can you imagine that? How would you like to be caught in such a downpour?

How do you get the best effect – with a short question or a long sentence that turns into a question?

What else do you notice about using questions in that way?

Questions that the audience is not given the opportunity to answer are called rhetorical questions. 'Can you imagine that?' is an example.

When you have finished writing your contrasting paragraphs, read them out to each other and ask the others to identify where you have used short sentences, exclamations, or rhetorical questions.

**Key concept**

### Sentence length

Good writers vary the length and type of their sentences (always remembering to put full stops at the ends of sentences). They use short sentences, exclamations, and rhetorical questions where they make the best effects. You have to judge when to use them – if you use too many, it breaks up the flow of your writing.

## A mother's complaint

This is a letter written to *Mothers and Children* in response to its article on page 132.

### Is television tremendous?

Dear Editor

I was reading the article called 'TV worldwide!' and **OK**, it's true what it says. But I was wondering if you other mums felt as I do about TV.

One thing – **kids** spend far too much time **gawking** at the screen when they should be out and about in the fresh air playing some kids' games and keeping healthy. You see, I don't think they take a lot of notice of poverty and suffering, or for that matter ecology. After all, politicians and scientists don't do much about it, do they, so how can you expect children to?

So what do they watch? Those teenage comedy dramas over and over again? The storylines are all right and the scripts not bad, but have you seen the appalling acting? They ought to call it 'Troublesome TV' really because you get the same old **diet**. There's a lot of so-called drama which is really miserable **stuff** about people with illnesses. There's an **awful** lot of police drama – do we really want our kids to have a diet of crime?

As kids grow up they will want to watch programmes made for an older audience, so I'd like them to see dramas about people from a poor background who do well in life – perhaps a lad who likes football and is discovered and gets to play professional – something positive to give kids a bit of hope.

Then there are those commercials. I guess young people like them because they are short, but they don't teach you concentration, do they? Ten minutes into a programme and you're interrupted by some person going on about her hair or worse still some horrible over-priced plastic toy. Not good. And I can never get to grips with the small print like '72% of 97 agree!' What sort of arithmetic is that?

So I think TV has quite a lot of work to do. If we mums ran it, who knows what we would do?

Scarlett Ryan

Fruity Hill, New South Wales

**Word cloud**

| | |
|---|---|
| awful | kids |
| diet | OK |
| gawking | stuff |

**Glossary**

**you other mums** Mothers like me who are reading this letter

**out and about** outside and free to roam

**all right** satisfactory, although not outstandingly good

**going on about** repeatedly talking about

## Understanding

1. What reason does Ms Ryan give for young people's lack of interest in poverty and suffering?
2. What sorts of programme and viewing does Ms Ryan think young people enjoy?
3. What does Ms Ryan not like about TV?
4. Ms Ryan says, 'If we mums ran it, who knows what we would do?' Role-play a meeting of mums (and/or dads). Discuss how you would make TV programmes suitable for young people. As you discuss, consider Ms Ryan's views on TV.

## Developing your language – creating a sense of audience

1. Think about who you are writing for when you write a story, an article, or a letter. Discuss how you might vary your language.
2. Write the beginning of a letter to your headteacher suggesting an improvement to your school meals. Discuss the type of language required.
3. Write the beginning of an email to a friend inviting her/him to the greatest party ever. Discuss how your language is different.
4. Read out your openings to the letter and the email and list the differences in the language.
5. Look back at Ms Ryan's letter and the article 'TV worldwide!' and compare the similarities and differences in the language.
6. Look at the way Ms Ryan uses the word 'awful'. Rewrite her sentence in a formal way.

## Word builder

**Write a formal version of each of the words in the Word cloud by answering the questions below.**

1. What would you say instead of 'as kids grow up'?
2. Re-write 'OK, it's true what it says'.
3. Replace the word 'stuff' in 'really miserable stuff'.
4. Replace the word 'gawking', which is a dialect word. The meaning is clear from the context.
5. Find a better way of saying 'the same old diet'.

## Antecedents and relative pronouns

What's wrong with these sentences?

> President Alkira gave President Alkira's speech to the assembly.
>
> My mother's favourite possession is my mother's grandmother's green vase.

If you said 'clumsy' you'd be right, so try re-writing them using the pronouns 'his' and 'her'.

> President Alkira realised that his life was in danger.

'President Alkira' is the **antecedent** for the pronoun 'his'.

**Identify the antecedent and pronoun in these sentences.**

> My parents were very proud of their hard-working children.
>
> Mariam, my sister, and I are very fond of our friendly pet snake.

**Remember**

A **pronoun** is a word that replaces a noun, e.g. *I*, *you*, and *which*.

When 'its' is a pronoun, there is no apostrophe between the 't' and the 's'.

### Singular or plural?

Look at this example.

> Each one of the girls scored a high mark in her test.

'Each one' is a singular antecedent and is replaced by a singular pronoun, 'her'.

> The juicy mango tempts my taste buds as it sits on the table.

'Juicy mango' is the antecedent and is replaced by a singular pronoun, 'it'.

An antecedent is the person or thing to which the pronoun refers back.

**Fill in the gaps with the correct pronouns. Be careful to find the antecedent and to work out whether it is singular or plural.**

1. Alfredo and Enri were the highest scorers in ______ tests.
2. The President of the Republic gave ______ inaugural speech to the parliament.
3. Some valuable items have been stolen from ______ case.
4. Each of my sisters asked for a reward for ______ hard work.

**Correct the incorrect pronouns in these sentences.**

5. The new teacher carrying a pile of books lost their balance at the entrance to the classroom.
6. These boys were thoughtless and have all disgraced the name of their school.
7. Both of the new pilots took charge of his plane for a passenger flight.

## Relative pronouns

**Answer the following questions.**

**1. a** What don't you like about these two sentences?

I talked to your teacher. He told me about your unfinished homework.

Would this be better, and why?

I talked to your teacher, who told me about your unfinished homework.

**b** Join up these two sentences to make them flow better.

I like going out with my Dad. He always finds me something interesting to do.

**2.** Now look at a different type.

This is my favourite photo. It shows you the beach and the palm trees.

A photo is a thing, so:

This is my favourite photo, which shows you the beach and the palm trees.

**Fill in the gaps with the correct relative pronouns.**

**a** I did some shopping for my next door neighbour ______ has been very unwell.

**b** I can't do this homework ______ is far too difficult for me.

**c** I've reached the last few pages of the story ______ I find very sad.

**Remember**

A **relative pronoun** does what it says – it takes an idea and relates it to a person or a thing. Be careful, though – you have to use 'who' for people and 'which' for things.

**3.** Now consider how we use 'whose' to join up sentences.

I like going to see my friend. His computer games are better than mine.

Joined together they become:

I like going to see my friend whose computer games are better than mine.

**Use the possessive form of 'who' to join these sentences.**

**a** I met the famous writer. His stories about dinosaurs have been bestsellers.

**b** I shall keep out of the way of my angry sister. Her tempers are not to be experienced.

**4.** What's wrong with the following sentence?

I'm lucky to have so many friends which are really good to me.

## A choir steps out

harmony
intonation
pitch
repertoire
rhythmically
volume

### Glossary

**loads of crime** (informal) a great amount of crime

**sort of transfixed** (informal) as if they could not move from their seats

**went from strength to strength** we made great progress

**it brought the house down** our performance was greeted by very loud and long applause and cheering

## Understanding

1. Why was the choir formed in the first place?
2. What difficulties did the choir face before it could leave on its tour?
3. What did the audience at the big concert like the most about what they saw and heard?
4. What did Mr Mhlongo do to make sure the choir sang well and believed in themselves?
5. What did the agent do for the choir and its members?
6. What were the benefits of the tour to the township?
7. Re-tell the story of the choir and its trip abroad in no more than six sentences.
8. Now look at this brief extract from the transcript. It includes some notes on what viewers might see as they watch the documentary. Work together to make a list of film shots you would want to include during the TV broadcast.

Charlize: Well, it's Mr Mhlongo. From the start he knew how to get us singing rhythmically – and moving. And he never seemed to have a cross word – always encouragement, encouragement. He made us lively, disciplined – the stepping moves are pretty complex and we swing our arms in patterns so our audiences are sort of transfixed. You see, like this – and like this.

## Developing your language – looking at specialised language

The words in the Word cloud are all semi-technical words to do with how choirs sing and what they sing. They are words you might need if you were writing about singing and they make your writing more powerful.

For example, 'rhythmically' tells you that an audience would expect to share a sense of beat and movement when the choir sang.

1. Research the subjects below.
   - Different types of bridge: beam bridge, arch bridge, cantilever bridge, suspension bridge, aqueduct
   - Parts of a car: radiator, distributor, shock absorber, camshaft, piston
   - Weather: cold front, anticyclone, hurricane, isobars, precipitation
2. Use books or the Internet to find five words you might need if you were writing about:

   Dinosaurs Acting Bones of the body Football

## Word builder

1. If someone in the audience said 'I couldn't hear them very well, there would be something wrong with their ______. (Choose a word from the Word cloud.)
2. If someone in the choir sang lower than everyone else, she would be singing at the wrong ______.
3. Explain why 'harmony' would be a good word to make part of the name for a choir.
4. How do you think you can sing rhythmically?
5. Explain why a choir giving a concert would have to have a good repertoire and what it might consist of.
6. What is the difference between having imperfect intonation and singing out of tune?

## Developing your language – using specialist language

Write the words of a short talk you could give about acting, football, or dinosaurs. Include the words you discovered when you researched the topics.

## Writing an article

You are going to write an article giving information and your views about a topic, for publication in a newspaper or magazine.

Read the article 'TV worldwide!' once more to remind you of how it was constructed and the language the writer used. Was the language entirely formal? Was it chosen with a particular audience in mind?

## Planning time

### What topic will you choose?

Choose a topic to do with school, or your town, or something you do as a pastime. If you have taken part in a sporting activity, you could write about your enjoyment of the sport. Alternatively, if you have been in a school play or concert, you could write about acting or playing a musical instrument.

If possible, choose a topic that you know a lot about and/or you feel strongly about/find really interesting.

### Who is your audience?

If you choose a school publication, who are you writing for? If you choose a local newspaper, how is your audience different?

### Thinking about your language and style

How formal or informal should your language be? Even in a school publication, the teachers will read what you write!

What effects might you be able to achieve by using longer sentences mixed with short sentences?

How can you make your language persuasive by addressing your audience directly?

### What is your title going to be?

How will you get the theme of your article across? How will you attract attention?

## Structuring your article

'TV worldwide!' was in four paragraphs, some of them not very long. Four paragraphs might be a good number to aim for.

### A first paragraph that attracts attention

Which of these would appeal to you as the first sentence?

'This article is about our school dinners.'

'Have you ever stopped to wonder, as you see all the juniors rushing to the dining hall, how good school dinners actually are?'

'I think they're a load of rubbish, they're not OK at all.'

Decide on an opening sentence then build an interesting descriptive paragraph from it.

### Paragraph 2: Get your theme across

How do you link the last sentence from the first paragraph to the first of the second?

Here's an example: 'Of course, not every football match is as exciting or easy as the one I've just described…'

What are you trying to persuade your audience to think and how can you be clear about it?

### Paragraph 3: Give some examples and vary your material

How do you make sure that you don't get stuck on one idea?

Here's an example: 'The rehearsals came to an end and suddenly it was the first performance. Nerves took over with a vengeance!'

And another: 'So far I've been very complimentary about my favourite meals, but I have one or two suggestions that could bring joy to my friends.'

### Paragraph 4: How do I end?

You could sum up your argument, but that is sometimes rather boring. Here are some ways you could begin the last paragraph.

'Looking back on my part on the play, my emotions are still very mixed, but I would recommend joining in a production.'

'The job of preparing meals for all of us hungry students must be a daunting one, and our kitchen staff are very devoted and do not always get the thanks they deserve.'

# Progress check ✓

1. Explain the difference between a TV soap and a TV documentary. [2 marks]
2. What two languages do most long words in English come from? [2 marks]
3. Give two examples of when you would use an exclamation mark. [2 marks]
4. What is a rhetorical question? Give an example. [2 marks]
5. When you write, how does your sense of audience affect the language you use? What language would you use if you were writing an email to your best friend? [2 marks]
6. What does the word 'antecedent' mean? Explain the relationship between an antecedent and a pronoun, and write a sentence to give an example. [4 marks]
7. Ms Scarlett Ryan had four objections to commercials on TV. What were they? [4 marks]
8. Suggest four specialised words that you might use if you were writing about the weather. [4 marks]
9. What is a relative pronoun? Which pronoun do you use for people, which for things, and which is possessive? [4 marks]
10. What four things do you think the girls' choir had to learn in order to sing properly? [4 marks]

## Reflecting on your learning

Choose the statement that is most appropriate in each case.

1. Do I understand that if I learn the meanings of prefixes they will help me to work out the meaning of words and to spell them?

   *I'm quite confident, thank you!*

   *Yes, but I need more practice.*

   *I still need someone to explain to me.*

2. Do I understand how to use exclamation marks and rhetorical questions?

   *I'm quite confident, thank you!*

   *Yes, but I need more practice.*

   *I still need someone to explain to me.*

3. Did I understand the work on antecedents?

   *Completely.* *Partially.* *I need more explanation.*

4. Did I understand the work on relative pronouns?

   *Completely.* *Partially.* *I need more explanation.*

5. Do I understand how I can vary the sort of language I use to suit an audience and write more or less formally?

   *Yes, I understand, and I try to do it already.*

   *I understand but have not practised it much.*

   *I need more help with this.*

6. Do I feel happy about varying my sentence lengths to write more effectively?

   *Yes, and I try to do it already.*

   *I understand but I have not practised it much.*

   *I need more help and more practice.*

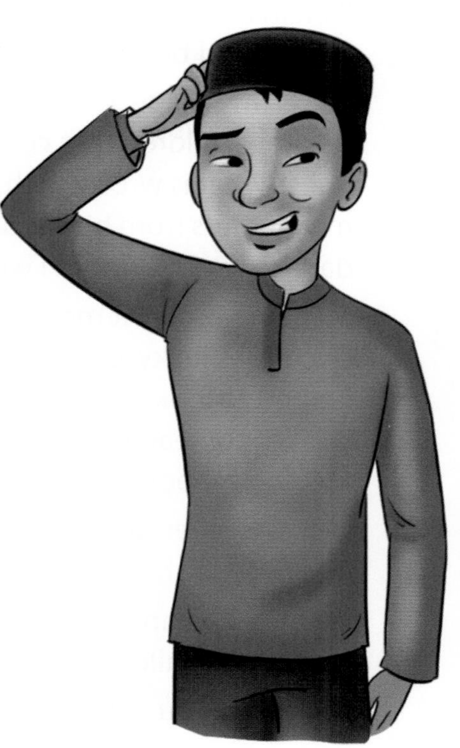

**Focus on your weaker areas. Think of how to improve these areas.**

- I'm happy that I understand most of what I have learned in the chapter. What can I do now to fill any gaps in my knowledge?
- What advice can I ask for and what practice do I need to do in my weaker areas over the next few weeks?
- What advice can I ask for and what practice do I need to do so that I'm confident I understand and use what I've learned?

This is an extract from *Sky Hawk* by Gill Lewis. If you're feeling confident with your reading, have a go at reading this extract before answering the Understanding questions on p149.

*Sky Hawk* is set in a small farming village in the mountains of Scotland. In this extract, Iris (an osprey) divides her time between Scotland and Africa. Iris migrates to Africa with a tracking device and Callum, the 11-year-old narrator of the story, finds a little girl who tries to help him look after the osprey. Iris unites two children from two very different countries.

## Sky Hawk

From: Jeneba Kah
Sent: 12th October 21.30 GMT
Subject: Iris

Hello Callum

Tell Rob I haven't been fighting with any crocodiles, but I'll remember to stick one in the eye if I ever do.

I am in hospital because I was hit by a truck. It skidded in the mud in the rainy season and broke my legs. I am in plaster waiting for them to mend.

I miss my village, but it is not so bad here in the hospital. I make friends with the new children that come into the ward. I pretend I am a doctor and try to guess what is wrong with them. In the evening Max sits on my bed and shows me pictures from his medical text books. He knows I want to be a doctor one day. He says he hopes I won't be as scary as Mama Binta though.

Mariama brought me some school work and chicken Yassa today, so I am two times lucky. Chicken Yassa is her special recipe, my favourite. Mariama helped to look after me when I was little after my mother died, but she is also our school teacher too. I did an hour of maths with her. It was so much fun. Missing school is the worst thing about being in hospital.

Max has taken some pictures of my village to send to you. I hope you like the one of the fish my little brother caught for Iris.

What is Scotland like? Max said it is cold and wet and people only eat something called haggis. What is haggis anyway?

I will send you news of Iris every day.

Your friend

Jeneba

I showed Rob and Euan the email and photos next day at school.

'She's crazy,' said Rob. 'I'd go and break my legs just to have time *off* school.'

'Now that's what I call a fish,' said Euan. 'Imagine **hauling** that in.'

The photo showed a young boy no older than seven or eight holding up a long silver fish. The boy had to stand on tiptoes to keep the tail off the floor.

I flicked over the other pictures. Max had taken photos of Jeneba's village. There were lots of small round huts and red brick buildings set around an open enclosure. The sky looked deep, deep blue, and the earth looked rust-red, dry and dusty. Under a fat-bellied tree sat a group of men hidden by the shade. In the open sunlight, women in brightly patterned clothes laid out fruits and vegetables to sell.

The last one was of Iris in Max's shed.

'It explains why we can't get a signal from Iris,' said Euan, 'if she's in a dark shed.'

'You can actually see the **transmitter** on her back and the long aerial poking out,' said Rob. 'She'd be dead by now if it wasn't for that.'

I nodded. 'She'll get better now,' I said, 'I just know she will.'

'We could send Jeneba some photos of Scotland,' said Euan.

'That's a great idea. We can take a photo of Iris's nest,' I said. 'I'll ask Mum to lend us her camera after school.'

Mum was in the kitchen doing the farm accounts at the table. She handed us the small digital camera she kept in her handbag. 'Make sure you take some of yourselves,' she said. 'Jeneba will want to know what you look like.'

Graham leaned across the table and helped himself to another huge piece of chocolate cake. 'She doesn't want to see Callum's ugly mug,' he said, dropping sticky crumbs over the accounts. 'It might crash the computer again. I'm surprised they have computers out in Uganda anyway.'

'The Gambia,' I said. 'Everywhere's got computers now.'

haul
preen
transmit

## Glossary

**aerial** a wire or rod that receives or transmits radio or television signals

**eyrie** the nest of an eagle or other bird of prey

**haggis** a Scottish dish made from sheep's offal, boiled in a skin with suet and oatmeal

**mug** (informal) a person's face

**to have a fit** (informal) to be very shocked or angry

Mum flicked the crumbs from the papers. 'You're not doing much at the moment are you, Graham? Make yourself useful and take Callum and his friends out in the Land Rover to take photos of the farm before it gets dark.'

Graham rolled his eyes. 'Come on then,' he said. He picked up the Land Rover keys and headed out of the door.

Graham took us all over the farm. We were suddenly rally drivers. I'm sure Mum would've had a fit if she'd seen some of his handbrake turns.

But we did get some great photos of the farm. Graham took a picture of us with the mountains in the background and I photographed Iris's eyrie on the island in the loch. When we got back to the farmhouse, Mum had defrosted a haggis from the freezer for us and we photographed that too.

Later that evening, I downloaded the photos onto the computer and attached them to an email. I pressed the send button and our photos of Scotland went flying through cyberspace in a fraction of a second, all the way to Jeneba and Iris. All the way to Africa.

Each day after that, Jeneba wrote about Iris and sent more photos that Max had taken. Iris looked stronger as the days went by. Her feathers became shiny and glossy. There was a picture of her standing on a piece of wood, **preening**. It had to be a good sign. The old wound on her foot looked better too. The first pictures showed a thick lump of red flesh caked in dirt and the skin of her foot had been mottled and dark. But now, nearly two weeks later, the pictures showed the wound had almost healed.

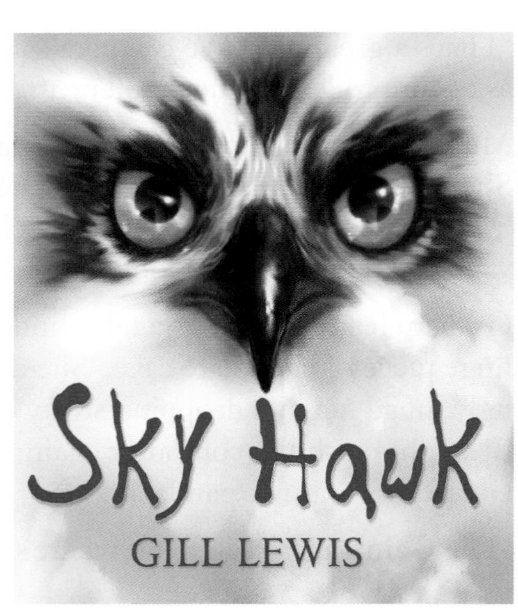


Max had also taken more photos and short video clips of the village and the river. It made me feel as if I was really there. I could almost imagine myself walking down to the wide green river, where the long wooden fishing boats lay on the low tide mud. I could almost feel the hot African sun on my face and hear the sounds of the village, of children playing and women pounding sorghum and millet. I was almost there.

Almost.

That night there was one more email waiting for me.

From: Jeneba Kah
Sent: 25th October 20.40 GMT
Subject: Iris

Hello Callum

Tomorrow is a very good day. Max has decided to set Iris free. He says she is strong now and needs to go back to the wild. He is going to release her at sunrise so she has the whole day to catch fish.

Doctor Jawara said he is taking the casts off my legs tomorrow, so I will be free too.

I am too excited to sleep. But Mama Binta said if I go to sleep she will let me see Max release Iris tomorrow. I think maybe Mama Binta isn't as fierce as she pretends to be.

I will write with good news tomorrow night.

Your friend, Jeneba.

## Understanding

1. Explain how the writer hooks in the reader with this chapter opener?
2. This chapter contains two different text types:
   - **a** What are the differences in style and language? Explain your answer.
   - **b** What do these bring to the chapter? Explain your answer.
3. **a** How does the writer describe the two settings?
   - **b** How are the two settings very different to one another? Explain your answer.
4. The two children come from very different communities. How do they connect?
5. The extract on page 150 contains yet another text type which can be found in the book. Callum's first-person narrative is occasionally paralleled by the osprey's own experience, as Callum imagines it.
   - **a** How is this diary entry presented to look different to the other text types?

b How does the author use the senses to describe the bird?

c Why do you think the writer includes details of the tracking device?

6. Write an exciting ending to the story using the techniques and text types that this writer has used.

| | |
|---|---|
| **blow** | **glare** |
| **brittle** | **oil** |

## Glossary

**loch** a lake in Scotland

**NASA** the National Aeronautics and Space Administration

**nostrils** the two openings in the nose

**sand-dunes** mounds of loose sand shaped by the wind

**swamp** a marsh

```
11th September
5.30 GMT
Sahara Desert
31°30′08.84″ N  0°41′37.21″ E
Speed: 0 km/h
Total distance: 3812.02 km
```

*Iris opened her eyes and ruffled her feathers. A pale orange dawn was spreading across the horizon. There were no landmarks to be seen, no green-lined oasis or bright strip of river. There were only the pale golden dunes rolling endlessly into the distance.*

*The sandstorm had raged all day and all night. It had **blown** Iris far into the desert where she found shelter beneath an outcrop of rock. Gritty sand had worked its way into her mouth and nostrils and rubbed on the soft skin beneath the downy feathers. One foot was swollen and ached where the old cut lay open, and her long flight feathers were dry and **brittle** from the heat. She started preening them, **oiling** them so the barbs on each were smooth and sealed again.*

*As the sun flared into the sky, Iris launched herself up into the rising spirals of air. All day she drifted southwards and westwards. The desert sun burned into her back and the midday sand **glared** bright in her eyes. As the sun curved down towards the horizon, Iris sank down with it through the cooling layers of air.*

*Below, a trail of camels and people trudged over the high dune ridges, their long dark shadows pressed against the golden sand. A child riding high on one of the camels pointed to her as she passed. Deep within Iris, the memories of the distant coldlands flowed through her, memories of a child watching, of rich fishing grounds and deep waters. They lifted her and carried her higher. And in the fading light a green smudge of trees and scrubland appeared, and beyond that, at last a strip of sunset reflected in the curves of a wide flowing river.*

I plotted Iris's journey in my diary over the following weeks and downloaded photos of some of the places she had flown across. One was the bizarre Richat Structure in Mauritania, a pattern of huge circles in the desert that NASA scientists could see from space. She flew across towns with strange names such as Ksar el Barka and Boutilimit. There were photos of whole villages gradually being swallowed up by huge sand-dunes and photos of camel trains heading into pale desert dawns.

Iris's flight took her south and west into Senegal and on to The Gambia. Her long migration came to an end along the banks of the River Gambia, not far from its opening to the sea. I looked at photos of the area. Dense green mangrove swamps and palms came down to the water's edge. Crocodiles slept on domed mud banks at low tide. Fishermen mended nets alongside brightly painted boats.

```
23rd September
08.00
Mangrove swamp, The Gambia
13°16′28.05″ N  16°28′58.14″ W
Speed: 0 km/h
Total distance: 6121.23 km
```

It was so different from the lochs and mountains of Scotland. And it had only taken her thirty-nine days to travel all the way. Hamish said some ospreys they had tracked made the flight in much less time.

Each day after that, Iris's signals came from the same area. Her flight pattern made zigzags across a small river inlet where she fished, to roost trees in the riverbanks. She seemed settled and I didn't check her position so often. I would have to wait until March before she started her migration north to Scotland again.

I sat down at the computer in my bedroom to check on her position. I hadn't logged on for a couple of days. I turned on the computer, ready to tap in Iris's code.

A stone pinged against my bedroom window.

I opened the window to see Rob and Euan in the yard below on their bikes.

From *Sky Hawk* by Gill Lewis

## Language and literacy reference

**Active voice versus passive voice** – Verbs are active when the subject of the sentence (the agent) does the action. Example: The shark swallowed the fish. Active verbs are used more in informal speech or writing.

Verbs are passive when the subject of the sentence has the action done to it. Example: The fish was swallowed by the shark. Passive verbs are used in more formal writing such as reports. Examples: An eye-witness was interviewed by the police. Results have been analysed by the sales team.

Sometimes turning an active sentence to passive, or vice versa, simply means moving the agent:

- The shark (agent and subject) + verb = active
- The fish (object) + verb = passive

**Adjective** – An adjective describes a noun or adds to its meaning. They are usually found in front of a noun. Example: Green emeralds and glittering diamonds. Adjectives can also come after a verb. Examples: It was big. They looked hungry. Sometimes you can use two adjectives together. Example: tall and handsome. This is called an adjectival phrase.

Adjectives can be used to describe degrees of intensity. To make a comparative adjective you usually add –er (or use more). Examples: quicker; more beautiful. To make a superlative you add –est (or use most). Examples: quickest; most beautiful.

**Adverb** – An adverb adds further meaning to a verb. Many are formed by adding -ly to an adjective. Example: slow/slowly. They often come next to the verb in a sentence. Adverbs can tell the reader: how – quickly, stupidly, amazingly; where – there, here, everywhere; when – yesterday, today, now; how often – occasionally, often.

**Adverbial phrase** – The part of a sentence that tells the reader when, where or how something happens is called an adverbial phrase. It is a group of words that functions as an adverb. Example: I'm going to the dentist **tomorrow morning** (when); The teacher spoke to us **as if he was in a bad mood** (how); Sam ran **all the way home** (where). These adverbials are called adverbials of time, manner and place.

**Alliteration** – Alliteration occurs when two or more nearby words start with the same sound. Example: A slow, sad, sorrowful song.

**Antecedent** – An antecedent is the person or thing to which the pronoun refers back. Example: President Alkira realised that his life was in danger. 'President Alkira' is the antecedent here.

**Antonym** – An antonym is a word or phrase that means the opposite of another word or phrase in the same language. Example: shut is an antonym of open. Synonyms and antonyms can be used to add variation and depth to your writing.

**Audience** – The readers of a text and/or the people for whom the author is writing; the term can also apply to those who watch a film or to television viewers.

**Clause** – A clause is a group of words that contains a subject and a verb. Example: I ran. In this clause, I is the subject and ran is the verb.

**Cliché** – An expression, idiom or phrase that has been repeated so often it has lost its significance.

**Colloquial language** – Informal, everyday speech as used in conversation; it may include slang expressions. Not appropriate in written reports, essays or exams.

**Colon** – A colon is a punctuation mark (:) used to indicate an example, explanation or list is being used by the writer within the sentence. Examples: You will need: a notebook, a pencil, a notepad and a ruler. I am quick at running: as fast as a cheetah.

**Conjugate** – To change the tense or subject of a verb.

**Conditional tense** – This tense is used to talk about something that might happen. Conditionals are sometimes called 'if' clauses. They can be used to talk imaginary situations or possible real-life scenarios. Examples: If it gets any colder the river will freeze. If I had a million pounds I would buy a zoo.

**Conjunction** – A conjunction is a word used to link clauses within a sentence such as: and, but, so, until, when, as. Example: He had a book in his hand when he stood up.

**Connectives** – A connective is a word or a phrase that links clauses or sentences. Connectives can be conjunctions. Example: but, when, because. Connectives can also be connecting adverbs. Example: then, therefore, finally.

**Continuous tense** – This tense is used to tell you that something is continuing to happen. Example: I am watching football.

**Discourse markers** – Words and phrases such as on the other hand, to sum up, however, and therefore are called discourse markers because they mark stages along an argument. Using them will make your paragraphs clearer and more orderly.

**Exclamation** – An exclamation shows someone's feelings about something. Example: What a pity!

**Exclamation mark** – An exclamation mark makes a phrase or a short sentence stand out. You usually use it in phrases like 'How silly I am!' and more freely in dialogue when people are speaking. Don't use it at the end of a long, factual sentence, and don't use it too often.

**Idiom** – An idiom is a colourful expression which has become fixed in the language. It is a phrase which has a meaning that cannot be worked out from the meanings of the words in it. Examples: 'in hot water' means 'in trouble'; It's raining cats and dogs.

**Imagery** – A picture in words, often using a metaphor or simile (figurative language) which describes something in detail: writers use visual, aural (auditory) or tactile imagery to convey how something looks, sounds or feels in all forms of writing, not just fiction or poetry. Imagery helps the reader to feel like they are actually there.

**Irregular verb** – An irregular verb does not follow the standard grammatical rules. Each has to be learned as it does not follow any pattern. For example, catch becomes caught in the past tense, not catched.

**Metaphor** – A metaphor is a figure of speech in which one thing is actually said to be the other. Example: This man is a lion in battle.

**Non-restrictive clause** – A non-restrictive clause provides additional information about a noun. They can be taken away from the sentence and it will still make sense. They are separated from the rest of the sentence by commas (or brackets). Example: The principal, who liked order, was shocked and angry.

**Onomatopoeia** – Words that imitate sounds, sensations or textures. Example: bang, crash, prickly, squishy.

**Paragraph** – A group of sentences (minimum of two, except in modern fiction) linked by a single idea or subject. Each paragraph should contain a topic sentence. Paragraphs should be planned, linked and organised to lead up to a conclusion in most forms of writing.

**Parenthetical phrase** – A parenthetical phrase is a phrase that has been added into a sentence which is already complete, to provide additional information. It is usually separated from other clauses using a pair of commas or a pair of brackets (parentheses). Examples: The leading goal scorer at the 2014 World Cup – James Rodiguez, playing for Columbia – scored five goals. The leading actor in the film, Hollywood great Gene Kelly, is captivating.

**Passive voice** – See active voice.

**Person (first, second or third)** – The first person is used to talk about oneself – I/we. The second person is used to address the person who is listening or reading – you. The third person is used to refer to someone else – he, she, it, they.

- I feel like I've been here for days. (first person)
- Look what you get, when you join the club. (second person)
- He says it takes real courage. (third person)

**Personification** – Personification can work at two levels: it can give an animal the characteristics of a human, and it can give an abstract thing the characteristics of a human or an animal. Example: I was looking Death in the face.

**Prefix** – A prefix is an element placed at the beginning of a word to modify its meaning. Prefixes include: dis-, un-, im-, in-, il-, ir-. Examples: impossible, inconvenient, irresponsible.

**Preposition** – A preposition is a word that indicates place (on, in), direction (over, beyond) or time (during, on) among others.

**Pronoun** – A pronoun is a word that can replace a noun, often to avoid repetition. Example: I put the book on the table. It was next to the plant. 'It' refers back to the book in first sentence.

- Subject pronouns act as the subject of the sentence: I, you, he, she, it.
- Object pronouns act as the object of the sentence: me, you, him, her, it, us, you, them.
- Possessive pronouns how that something belongs to someone: mine, yours, his, hers, its, ours, yours, theirs.
- Demonstrative pronouns refer to things: this, that, those, these.

**Questions** – There are different types of questions.

- Closed questions – This type of question can be answered with a single-word response, can be answered with 'yes' or 'no', can be answered by choosing from a list of possible